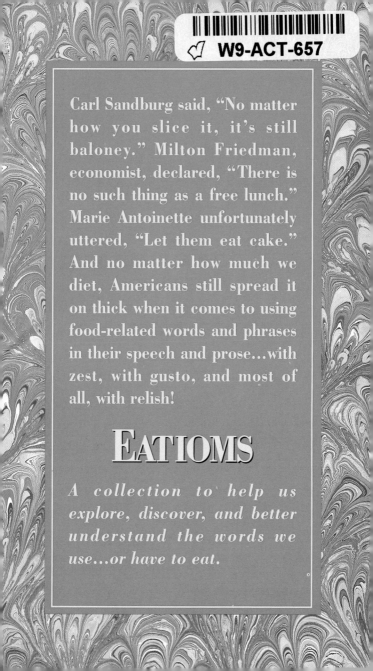

Carl Sandburg said, "No matter how you slice it, it's still baloney." Milton Friedman, economist, declared, "There is no such thing as a free lunch." Marie Antoinette unfortunately uttered, "Let them eat cake." And no matter how much we diet, Americans still spread it on thick when it comes to using food-related words and phrases in their speech and prose...with zest, with gusto, and most of all, with relish!

EATIOMS

A collection to help us explore, discover, and better understand the words we use...or have to eat.

DO YOU KNOW THAT . . .

"Slush fund" has nothing to do with ice and snow, but with the diets of sailors.

"To eat humble pie" is not only demeaning, it was an unappetizing dish of entrails served to servants.

"Moxie" is not Yiddish, but slang born in the U.S. of A.—as the name of a New England soft drink.

"Goober grease," derived from the Congolese word for *peanut*, is . . . peanut butter.

AND THAT THE BEST THING SINCE
SLICED BREAD IS . . .

EATIOMS

EATIOMS

JOHN D. JACOBSON

A LAUREL BOOK
Published by
Dell Publishing
a division of
Bantam Doubleday Dell Publishing Group, Inc.
666 Fifth Avenue
New York, New York 10103

ISBN: 0-440-20887-4

Printed in the United States of America

Published simultaneously in Canada

March 1993

10 9 8 7 6 5 4 3 2 1

OPM

PREFACE

Who will eat the kernel must break the shell.

—John Grange

Most people are *nuts* about the origins of word and phrase idioms, but don't have the resources, inclination, or time to crack through the shells in which their fascinating stories are encased. I've spent a lifetime getting to the *kernel* of such expressions, and I've always been surprised that etymologists have yet to establish a special category for idioms related to eating. I've corrected this omission by coining the word *eatioms,* a neologism (new word) that blends *eat* and (id)*ioms.*

Eatioms is a book that offers a delicious *buffet* of those words and phrases so dear to the hearts and minds—as well as the stomachs—of the world's eaters. Eatioms are frequently humorous and always fascinating, not only to serious idiom lovers, but to all speakers who share the English language, its colorful expressions, and a love of food.

How did a mixed drink become known as a *cocktail*? What is the derivation of *cold shoulder*? Why are some masters of the culinary art described as *cordon bleu chefs*?

We all know that a *baker's dozen* is defined as thirteen items for the price of twelve. But did you know that it's the result of an English law of 1266, which penalized bakers who short-weighted loaves of bread? Discover how the thirteen loaves provided protection against this punitive law.

The average person has absolutely no idea of the charm contained in some of the most commonly used phrases or words. *Eatioms* provides intellectual nourishment for the hungry at heart. *Bon appétit!*

EATIOMS

addle/addleheaded/addlepated—An *addled* egg is a rotten one, and this description is derived from the Old English word *adela,* meaning filth or something that is rotten. The idea of a *bad egg* has long been connected with the condition of the human mind or head, probably due to the head's similarity in shape to an egg. *Addled,* accordingly, has developed the derogatory sense of someone who is mentally confused or muddled. In this same "rotten" vein are *addleheaded* and *addlepated,* both referring to someone who is lacking good sense.

ambrosia/nectar/nectarine—The classical gods of the Greeks and Romans had to be fed, too, according to the beliefs of that time. The mythological food and drink of the gods were called *ambrosia* and *nectar,* respectively. Both words remain in use today, but for less divine purposes than their etymologies would suggest. The word *ambrosia* is derived from two Greek elements, *am-,* meaning not, and *-brosos,* meaning mortal: literally, then, it refers to a substance for the immortals. *Nectar* is derived from the Greek element *nekros,* meaning dead, and the Sanskrit word *taras,* meaning victorious, and thus literally describes a victory over death.

Today, the word *nectar* is used to describe any delicious drink. The *nectarine,* which was first discovered in the early seventeenth century, is a mutation of the peach that has a smooth surface without the *peach fuzz.*

apple knocker—Throughout the centuries, farm workers have been held in low regard by their city cousins. Consider the following words, which started out innocently enough, but which later developed a derogatory sense: *heathen,* a person who lived in the heath (countryside); *pagan,* from the Latin word *pagus* (country); *rustic,* from the Latin word *rusticus* (country); *villain,* a farm worker, from the Latin word *villus* (farmstead); *boor,* from the Dutch word *boer* (peasant); *savage,* a variation of the Latin word *silva* (a wood or forest).

Today's reapers of the harvest, often poorly paid migrant workers, fare little better than their ancient counterparts. *Apple knocker,* an eatiom often applied to farm laborers, has a wide range of meanings including fruit picker, hick, unsophisticated person, and rural dweller. The term *apple knocker* was derived from the practice of knocking apples from trees with sticks, apparently a common method of harvesting that fruit.

apple of discord—The *Big Apple* (see *Apple, the Big*) is a golden apple for those who enjoy art, music, theater, and gourmet dining. It can also be an *apple of discord* when it comes to crime, drugs, violence, and the homeless. The phrase *apple of discord,* which can be traced back to classical Greek mythology, has come to mean anything that causes trouble, conflict, or jealousy.

According to the myth, it all began at the marriage of Thetus, which was attended by all the gods, when one of the deities, Discord, threw a golden apple on the table. The apple was inscribed with the words *For the most beautiful,* and was quickly claimed by three of the attending goddesses: Aphrodite, Athena, and Hera. The selection of the most beautiful was left to Paris, who awarded the gilded fruit to Aphrodite because she promised to help him kidnap Helen of Troy. These events brought on the Trojan War—along with a lot of discord.

apple of one's eye—In Anglo-Saxon times, the word *pupil* also meant apple, and the words were interchangeable. When members of these early Germanic tribes referred to a loved one, particularly a child or grandchild, as the *apple of my eye,* they were actually saying that the object of their affection was as valuable as the pupil of their own eye—or, simply, precious.

apple-pie order—How did *apple-pie order* become an eatiom meaning neat, prim, or proper? The phrase *apple-pie order* actually has nothing to do with pie, but is, rather, a misinterpretation of the French *nappe pliée,* folded linen.

applesauce / apple, Adam's / apple polisher / apple cart, upset the / apple, alley / apple, sad / apples, sour / apple-pie-and-motherhood—Too much of anything, even something as nutritious and as tasty as applesauce, isn't good. Proprietors and occupants of boardinghouses found that out the hard way. Because it was cheap, applesauce was frequently served to boarders in lieu of more expensive fare. As a result, applesauce became commonplace and was held in low regard. The word *applesauce,* therefore, suffered semantically as it developed a less respectable meaning, as was the case with *baloney* (which see). *Apple* is a toponym (a word derived from a place name) that comes from Abella, Italy, where apples grow in abundance. Here are some additional apple idioms for you to bite into:

Adam's apple—This is the name of a projection in the throat composed of cartilage, which is more prominent in men than in women. It is so called because of the superstition that a piece of the forbidden fruit eaten in the Garden of Eden lodged in Adam's throat.

apple polisher—This term designates a person who attempts to gain special favor from another by literally or figuratively polishing an apple in order to make it more attractive to its intended recipient.

upset the apple cart—to ruin or spoil someone's plans; to disrupt. The picture of an overturned apple cart with apples rolling in all directions should sufficiently explain the sense of this eatiom.

alley apple—a piece of horse manure.

sad apple—an unhappy or gloomy person.

sour apples—An eatiom used to express something done badly or unsuccessfully. (He can't sing for *sour apples.*)

apple-pie-and-motherhood—something deemed very virtuous; excellent.

Apple, Big—In the mid-1970s, the New York City Convention Bureau adopted the nickname the *Big Apple* for the city to replace its "Fun City" moniker, which had been adopted earlier. There are several theories for this juicy sobriquet, but we shall peel away the secondary origins and get right to the main core of this eatiom.

To the black jazz musicians of the Roaring Twenties, a club in Harlem known as the Big Apple was the most prestigious place to work. The Big Apple was also a popular dance craze of the

1930s; it was introduced, not surprisingly, at this same club. To play in the Big Apple was the goal of every jazz musician of the era. Eventually, the name the *Big Apple* was applied to the city itself.

bacchanal / Bacchanal / Bacchic / Bacchae—The
word *myth* is derived from a Greek word, *muthos,*
a speech or narrative. But myth can also mean an
unproved or false belief; for example, we now
look back upon what the ancients considered to
be serious religion as quaint pagan superstition.

Most of the Roman gods and goddesses were
fashioned after earlier Greek models. The Romans especially admired the Greek god of wine,
fertility, and drama—Dionysus. So fond were
they, in fact, that they took Dionysus' alternate
name, Bakkhos (which they spelled *Bacchus*) for
their own god of wine.

The Romans went one step further and held
annual feasts in honor of Bacchus, which they
called Bacchanalia. These celebrations turned out
to be wild orgies of eating and drinking. Bacchus
even had female attendants, called Bacchae. Today, *bacchanal* is lower-cased when referring to a
drunken reveler, and *bacchic* is still used to de-

scribe anything pertaining to or honoring *Bacchus,* a *Bacchanal,* or *bacchanal.*

bacon, bring home the—There are two explanations for this eatiom, which has come to mean to earn a living. One source attributes it to the centuries-old custom of conducting greased-pig contests at English fairs. In these matches, the person who caught the slippery swine received as his prize the right to *bring home the bacon.*

There is also the compelling legend of the noblewoman of Dunmow, England, who established the Dunmow flitch tradition. In this version, a happily married man could go to Dunmow, kneel before the church on designated stones, and swear that for a year and a day he never once had a domestic quarrel with his spouse or ever wished that he was not married. Such a person could claim a flitch (side) of a pig as his prize for this feat.

There are those who claim that during a period of more than five hundred years no one came forward to *bring home the (Dunmow) bacon.* To this day, Dunmow flitch is synonymous with domestic bliss.

bacon, save one's—This "bacon" phrase has two possible origins, one from cant (thieves' slang) and one much older.

The first theory suggests that *bacon* was a cant word for boodle (a stolen object). The second theory holds that *bacon* was derived from the Anglo-Saxon word *bæc,* or a person's backside. The word *bæc* was transformed to bacon to describe the meat carved from the back of the hog. So, to *save one's bacon* came to mean to save one's back from getting a whipping; later, this was modified to mean to spare one from injury or loss.

baker's dozen—In medieval England a baker who sold anything but a full loaf in size or weight was severely punished. The *baker's dozen,* wherein thirteen items are sold for the price of twelve, was a practice developed by bakers of that period to protect themselves from prosecution. This old mathematical formula still has its proponents, and even in the mid-twentieth century selling thirteen cookies, doughnuts, or cupcakes for the price of twelve was a common practice in most bakeries. The *baker's dozen* concept was prevalent in other industries as well.

This quaint custom was an outgrowth of an English law enacted in 1266 under King Henry III, which penalized bakers who short-weighted loaves of bread. The thirteenth loaf was called the "vantage" (from advantage) loaf and is thought to have been the profit for the bread hucksters (vendors). In fairness to medieval bakers, it should be mentioned that maintaining uniform loaf size or weight in those primitive ovens must have been quite difficult.

The *baker's dozen* was probably the first of the quantity discounts found so often today in many industries. So you see, the *baker's dozen* was not such a *half-baked* idea after all. We can certainly understand the wisdom of the phrase *half a loaf is better than none,* but for a medieval baker, *half a loaf* could really get him burned.

baloney (also boloney and balony)—*Baloney* has, of course, become synonymous with nonsense and is used as an exclamation of scorn or rejection. But how did this sausage develop its negative sense? I shall present the case for *baloney* (or shall I say the baloney casing?).

Baloney is an anglicized version of *Bologna,* an Italian city renowned for its gastronomic delicacies. One of Bologna's specialties was its sausages made from chopped guts and cheap ground meat. Unlike *humble pie* (cattle intestines) and *sweetbreads* (cattle thymus or pancreas) (both of which see), baloney's unappetizing contents finally caught up with it and it took on its current negative meaning—because "no matter how you slice it, it's still baloney."

bananas, go / banana oil / banana, top / banana republic / banana seat—It's difficult to write about *bananas* without *going bananas,* because an etymologist can slip up pretty badly on these multiple banana origins. Our first surprise was the discovery that although the name for this fruit, *banana,* is reported to be from the Taino language of the Caribbean, the Arab word *banana* means toes and fingers. This must be more than a coincidence, and it has been suggested that after the Spaniards and Portuguese discovered the fruit and its Indian name, they transported it to Africa where the Arabs used it as a simile for human fingers and toes.

   go bananas—wild and crazy. This expression is of American origin from the 1960s. The official explanation for its special slang use is that bananas are bent, not straight. I suspect that its special sense is in part due to the wild spills that occur in cartoons and slapstick routines when someone slips on a banana peel.

banana oil—a sweet-smelling liquid derived from amyl alcohol extracted from the banana. Used primarily as a paint solvent, it has come also to mean nonsense.

top banana—a complimentary nickname for burlesque comedians who enjoyed top billing. The idiom is attributed to a burlesque comedian, Frank Lebowitz, a headliner, who used bananas in his act and became known as the "top banana," a term by which all other top comedians on the circuit were eventually known. In Lebowitz's case, though, his position as top banana could have been due to the *peals* of laughter that he created with his bananas. Today, a *top banana* is the top man, president, or *big enchilada* (which see).

banana republic—a derisive reference to a small tropical country, usually in the Western Hemisphere, whose economy is based on the export of fruits, the tourist trade, and investments by foreigners.

banana seat—a hard, long curved bicycle seat first used in the sixties.

banquet / **buffet** / **smorgasbord**—This *buffet* of words conjures up a vision of tables laden with a variety of delicious foods, but each of these words is used eatiomatically as well.

banquet—an elaborate meal; feast—from the Italian word *banchetto,* a little board or table upon which foods were served. This "table" sense of board is also observed in such terms as *chairman of the board,* a person who sat at the head of the board (table) in the chair of honor reserved for him, while the other participants sat on benches. *Banquet* is also used to suggest a visual or mental feast, such as a banquet of the soul.

buffet—a piece of furniture for storing dishes, silverware, and linens. It has been suggested that *buffet,* a word of French origin, originally described a table with a sideboard that could be lowered with a slap (buffet) of the hand. It later became synonymous with *smorgasbord*, and like *smorgasbord* has come to mean a variety or assortment of any kind.

smorgasbord—a wide variety of cheeses, fishes, meats, salads, and appetizers. *Smorgasbord* is of Swedish origin and combines *smorgas-*, meaning sandwich, and *-bord*, a table. *Smorgasbord* is often used eatiomatically to mean a variety or assortment.

barbecue—The *barbecue* is a truly American tradition, because this custom and the word by which it is known can be traced to the Taino Indian people and language of the American West Indies. On festival occasions the Tainos would roast a whole animal on a raised *barbacoa* or wooden platform. Today's *barbecue* involves a piece of meat, fish, or fowl being roasted over an open fire and frequently basted with *barbecue sauce*. *Barbecue* can also refer to any social or political get-together.

It may be of some interest here to explain the source of the word *buccaneer*, meaning a pirate, which can also be traced to the Caribbean. Originally, French settlers living in Haiti subsisted on *bocan,* from a South American word for a grill on which meats were either dried or cooked. Later, pirates used this same method of preparing meats and those who prepared *bocan* (also spelled *boucan*) became known as *buccaneers.*

Barmecide feast—*The Arabian Nights* is a collection of Eastern folk tales that probably came from Arabian, Indian, and Persian legends dating back a thousand years. These tales are also known as *The Arabian Nights' Entertainment,* or *A Thousand and One Nights.* One of these yarns describes a feast to which a starving man was invited by Prince Barmecide. Much to the hungry guest's chagrin, there was no food to be had at the so-called feast. A *Barmecide feast,* therefore, has come to mean an illusory banquet where no food is served, or any pretended hospitality or generosity.

bean / bean ball / bean, old / beans / beans, doesn't know much about / beans, not worth a hill of / beans, spill the / beans, full of / beanfeast (beanfest) / beanerie / bubkes—Beans are the edible and nourishing seeds of various plants of the legume family, particularly the genus *Phaesolus.*

Bean eatioms essentially fall into two categories: those that result from the bean's similarity to a person's head, and those based on the relatively low cost of the bean.

bean—slang for a person's head, as well as a coin or dollar bill.

bean ball—a baseball thrown by a pitcher with the intention of coming near to or hitting the batter's head. A person hit by a *bean ball* or any other object is said to be *beaned.*

old bean—an essentially British phrase used informally in addressing a chum.

beans—a slight amount of anything.

doesn't know (much about) beans—a reference to a person who knows little about a specific subject.

not worth a hill of beans—a thing or person of little value.

spill the beans—to disclose secret information and thereby ruin a surprise.

full of beans—This eatiom has two completely different meanings: to be energetic, a reference to the flatulence often caused by the consumption of beans; and to be stupid, erroneous, or uninformed.

beanfeast (also **beanfest**)—an annual party given by an employer for employees.

beanerie—a nickname for a cheap or inferior restaurant.

bubkes—something trivial; nothing. *Bubkes* is the Yiddish (via Russian) word for beans.

beefcake—The term *beefcake,* from the 1940s, was modeled on the expression *cheesecake* (which see) and is defined as photographs of muscular young men who pose in a seminude state.

Where the eatiom *cheesecake* hinged on the color similarity between cheesecake and the skin of pretty girls, the male counterpart, *beefcake,* substituted *beef-* for *cheese-,* a reference to the apparent strength of these men.

berry/berries, the—The berry, a product of nature's bounty, has been eagerly sought after by man and his evolutionary predecessors since the dawn of these fruits. It is, accordingly, a symbol of something good. The berry's popularity is expressed in such phrases as *it's the berries,* designating a thing or person that is unusually good, attractive, or satisfying. *Berry* is also a synonym for the dollar, because both the dollar and the berry are perceived as good. The word *berry* is, according to some authorities, derived from a Celtic word meaning red. Although red is indeed the color of many a berry, we also use the expression *as brown as a berry* to describe a person with a good suntan.

biscuit / biscuit, ground / biscuit-shooter (-roller) / biscuit, cold—This English word means different things depending on whether the speaker is British or American. To a Brit, a biscuit is an unleavened wafer, cracker, cookie, or hard roll, while to his American counterpart a biscuit is a leavened bread baked in small rolls. *Leaven,* incidentally, is derived from the Latin word *levare,* meaning to make light. Bread is leavened with baking soda, yeast, or any other raising agent (see *sourdough*).

The word *biscuit* derives from the Italian word *biscotti,* which has Latin roots, and means twice cooked. The double-baking definition suggests that it was originally made in a crisp, hard, unleavened form (like a dog biscuit). Its hardness made it an ideal nonperishable and easily transportable food supply for long journeys.

ground biscuit—a piece of horse manure.

biscuit-shooter (-roller)—a cook.

cold biscuit—a dull or homely woman.

borscht belt (circuit)—Many of the greatest American comedians of the twentieth century started their careers in the borscht belt, a lecture and entertainment circuit in the Catskill Mountains of New York, approximately one hundred miles north of the *Big Apple* (see *Apple, Big*). The so-called borscht belt consisted of a group of hotels in the region that catered to a predominantly Jewish clientele. Borscht, a soup made of beets and cabbage, often topped with sour cream, was frequently served at these hotels, and it was from this staple soup that the circuit derived its name.

Borscht comes from the Russian word *borshch,* meaning beet soup.

20

bread / bread, break / bread and butter / breadline / breadwinner / bread cast upon the waters / bread is buttered on, know which side one's / breadbasket / bread, best thing since sliced—Bread, the staff of life, has long been a symbol of sustenance and livelihood, and is mentioned in the Lord's Prayer, common to most Christian religions: "Give us this day our daily bread. . . ." Bread's importance in sustaining life has resulted in its becoming synonymous with money. There are those, however, who attribute the bread-and-money connection to the Cockney rhyming-slang ditty "bread and honey"—meaning money. The word *bread* comes from the Greek word *broutos,* which is associated with the fermentation process in liquor, beer, and leavened bread.

break bread—to eat.

bread and butter—something that is very basic.

breadline—a queue formed by those who are out of work and lack the money to buy food, and therefore must stand in a food line. The *breadline* has become a symbol of hard times, especially since the 1930s.

breadwinner—the person in a family unit who *brings home the bacon* (see *bacon, bring home the*).

bread cast upon the waters—an act of a spiritual or financial nature that will be returned many times.

know which side one's bread is buttered on—to understand those things or issues that are to one's advantage.

breadbasket—a person's stomach; a geographical reference to a region where wheat is grown, such as Iowa.

best thing since sliced bread—a person or thing that is outstanding.

brown, do it up / brown-bag—To *do it up brown* means to do something perfectly or thoroughly. This eatiom is derived from the kitchen, where the object of every good cook is to prepare certain foods, such as beef, biscuits, and bread, so that they achieve a delectable brown color appropriate to that particular food. This expression is applied more generally, nowadays, to anything that is done to perfection.

To *brown-bag* is another brown eatiom that simply means to take one's lunch to the office, or liquor to a restaurant, in the proverbial *brown bag*. One must be careful when *brown-bagging* at a restaurant, however, because the proprietor might get *browned off,* a British idiom meaning annoyed.

brunch—This hybrid eatiom was among the first of a special breed of words that are variously labeled as portmanteau, blend, telescope, and *brunch* words. One of these crossbreeds is attributed to Lewis Carroll (1832–1898), author of *Alice's Adventures in Wonderland* and other children's books, who coined *slithy,* a combination of *slimy* and *lithe.*

The term *brunch,* which combines *br(eakfast)* and *(l)unch,* can also be traced to a British author, in this case Tom Beringer, who coined it in 1895. It was first quoted in *Punch,* a British humor magazine, in 1896.

Brunch is any late-morning meal that combines typical breakfast and lunch foods, but more recently has become associated with sumptuous buffets served on Sundays, usually between 10:00 A.M. and 2:00 P.M.

23

bubble and squeak / bubblehead / bubble queen / bubble dancer / bubbly—The British fondness for unusual nicknames inspired the doubly echoic phrase *bubble and squeak*, their term for meat and greens (usually cabbage) that are first boiled together and then fried. *Bubble* is the sound made when this meat-and-veggie combo is boiled, and *squeak* describes the sound made when it is fried. *Bubble and squeak* in British eatiomology also describes something affected but of little value, such as a person's title or rank; it also designates a button or pin denoting club affiliations.

  bubblehead—a stupid person.

  bubble queen—a jocular term for a female laundry worker.

  bubble dancer—a dishwasher; a nude or seminude dancer who uses balloons (bubbles) in her act for cover.

  bubbly—as a noun, champagne; also used as an adjective to mean effervescent, enthusiastic.

bubble gummer/bubble-gum set/bubble-gum music—This sticky subject owes its success to the sap or chicle of the sapodilla tree, first discovered in Mexico and chewed by the natives there. Because of its popularity with the young, who seem to be uninhibited with regard to blowing bubbles, these eatioms pertaining to adolescents blew into view:

bubble gummer—a teenager (teenybopper).

bubble-gum set—children in their early teens.

bubble-gum music—music such as rock and roll that appeals to a *bubble-gummer*.

Incidentally, *bubble* is an echoic word (one that mimics sound), while *gum* is derived from an Egyptian word for the exudate, or gum, of the acanthus leaf.

buns / bun / buns, hot cross / bun in the oven, to have a—*Bun*, derived from the Irish word *boinneoq*, had the original sense of a swelling. The *hot cross bun* can be traced to the ancient Greeks, who offered these small sacramental cakes to Apollo, Diana, Hecate, and the moon. These cakes "with horns," according to Brewer's *Dictionary of Phrase and Fable*, were called *bous*, a Greek word meaning cow or bull. To the Greeks the cross represented the four quarters of the moon. It is reported that these special cakes, miraculously, never grew moldy.

At some point in the bun's long history, Christians adopted it, mistaking the cross design as the Christian cross. Cross buns became associated with, and were eaten on, Good Friday and throughout Lent. The cross is made with a milk glaze. From the word's "swelling" sense, *buns* has come to mean the buttocks. *Bun* is also used as a synonym for a state of drunkenness, as in the expression *to have a bun on. To have a bun in the oven* is said of a pregnant woman.

butcher / butcher shop / butcher wagon—A place where they butcher meat is not a pretty sight. In fact, such a place could be described as a shambles, the name used by the English for a butcher shop. *Shambles* was originally a stool or bench on which butchers cut meat, and eventually the word *shambles* became synonymous with a butcher shop itself. In the beautiful and ancient English city of York, in the former county of Yorkshire, there is a street called the Shambles, which was at one time a street of butcher shops, now replaced by fashionable boutiques. The word *shambles,* today, denotes a place of great disorder.

The term *butcher* is derived from the Greek word *bouthytes,* one who sacrifices an ox (*bous*).

butcher—As a noun this has come to mean an unskilled or sloppy surgeon, a savage ruler, or a sloppy worker; as a verb, *butcher* means to destroy or ruin something.

butcher shop—a hospital.

butcher wagon—an ambulance.

butter and egg man, big—The cholesterol-ridden phrase *big butter and egg man* has come to mean a prosperous businessman or farmer from a small town who comes to the big city to spend his money in a showy manner. It can be traced directly to a mistress of ceremonies, Texas Guinan, who owned a nightclub in New York City during the Roaring Twenties.

According to tradition, in 1924 a wealthy farmer came to the club and was so taken with the pretty show girls there that he gave half a C note (fifty dollars) to each of them. Texas Guinan, wishing to publicly thank the big spender, asked him who he was. He replied that he was in the dairy and poultry business, whereupon Guinan introduced him as "a big butter and egg man."

butter wouldn't melt in her mouth / butterball / butter bar / butter up / buttercup / butterfingers / butterflies—The word *butter* is derived from two ancient Greek word elements, *bous-,* meaning cow, and *-turos,* cheese, or the term *bous turos.*

> **butter wouldn't melt in her mouth**—said of a person (usually a girl or woman) who is so cool or innocent that butter wouldn't melt in her mouth because of her assumed lower-than-normal body temperature.

> **butterball**—a plump or fat person.

> **butter bar**—an army second lieutenant, so called because his insignia of rank, one gold bar, looks like a bar of butter.

> **butter up**—to flatter; soft-soap; praise.

> **buttercup**—an attractive young woman.

> **butterfingers**—a person who is clumsy or who drops things, such as a baseball player who drops a ball.

butterflies—the butterfly was so named because at one time a yellow butterlike variety was predominant. To "get butterflies" is to have an anxious feeling in the pit of the stomach.

cabbage/cabbagehead—Cabbage can be traced to the Latin word *caput,* meaning head, with a number of translations into other languages along the way. Cabbage is a synonym for the American dollar bill because of the greenish, cabbage-colored ink used to print its reverse side (see *lettuce*). A *cabbagehead* is an eatiom for a stupid person.

café / cafeteria / coffee klatsch / coffee grinder / coffeepot—Word origins based on legend have a special fascination. The origin of *coffee* presented here is based on an ancient legend that attributes coffee's discovery to a goatherd named Kaldi who lived in the town of Kaffa in what is now Ethiopia. Kaldi, according to this legend, was tending his flock one day when he noticed that his goats seemed to be overly stimulated after eating the beans of a bush that grew wild nearby. After eating these beans himself and enjoying the effect, Kaldi told his neighbors about it.

The beans, named after the town, Kaffa, which was translated into Arabic as *qahwah,* were first used as a medicine or food, later a wine, and finally the brewed drink we know today.

café/cafeteria—as *qahwah* worked its way westward to Italy, it became *caffè,* a word that was also used to describe a small shop where they sold caffè, and that was finally anglicized to *café,* a coffee shop. The American Spanish version of *café* was *cafeteria,* which eventually became the name for self-service restaurants.

coffee klatsch—a social gathering at which informal conversation and coffee are enjoyed.

coffee grinder—a striptease artist.

coffeepot—a lunch or coffee counter.

cake, let them eat—*"Qu'ils mangent de la brioche,"* which translates into English as "Let them eat cake," was attributed to Marie Antoinette (1755–1793). The queen's callous statement was reportedly her response to the news that the French peasantry had no bread and were starving. The "cake" quote did not originate with her, however, as the colloquialism had already been in use for many years.

cake, piece of / cakewalk / cake, take the / cake, icing (frosting) on the / beefcake / cheesecake / johnny-cake / cake-cutter / cake-eater—The word *cake* can be traced to the Dutch word *koek,* which is related to the English word *cook.* The diminutive of *koek* is *koekje,* a small cake or cookie.

> **piece of cake**—This idiom can be traced to World War II British fliers who used it to describe something easy or pleasant.

> **cakewalk**—During the slave era in the American South, blacks were permitted to conduct fancy walking contests. The contests consisted of a promenade by couples in which the pair of walkers with the most creative strut would win a cake. Such a contest became known as a cakewalk, now defined as something easy, certain, or sure. Modern tap dancing, according to common belief, was an outgrowth of these original cakewalks.

> **take the cake**—often said about someone who won a *cakewalk;* has come to mean to surpass

all others; to win the prize. There is evidence that a cake was a prize for outstanding performance in ancient times as well.

icing (frosting) on the cake—Anyone who's ever enjoyed licking the bowl of icing after baking a cake knows how this idiom has come to mean something special or something added to make the whole better.

beefcake—(which see). Also see *cheesecake*.

cheesecake—(which see).

johnnycake—a cake or bread made of corn meal, water, and milk, first cooked on hot stoves but now on a griddle. The name of this cake has a variety of explanations for its source including *journey cake, Shawnee cake,* and *jonakin* (thought to be a perversion of *Shawnee cake*). It is now most often baked in an oven or fried.

cake-cutter—a person who shortchanges another.

cake-eater—a ladies' man.

calorie/lo-cal/calorie counter—Antoine Lavoisier (1743–1794), who coined the word *carbohydrate* (which see), was the French scientific genius who theorized that food matter, when mixed with oxygen in the stomach, creates energy. This brings us to *calorie,* which is the scientific unit used to express the heat output of an organism and the fuel value of food. The word for *calorie* first came into use in France in about 1833 as *coloric,* but was corrected to *calorie* in 1866.

Calorie is derived, via the French, from the Latin word *calor,* meaning heat.

In the 1950s, a food that had a low calorie count was described as *lo-cal,* but this word gave way to *diet* as the descriptive adjective for such foods and drinks. A *calorie counter* is someone who is on a diet.

canapé—The canapé is defined as a piece of bread or toast on top of which caviar, anchovies, cheese, or other delectables are spread. A canopy, on the other hand, is a fabric draped on posts or suspended directly over a bed and presently used as a decorative device.

Both can be traced to the Greek word *konopeion,* meaning a mosquito netting, which was originally suspended over a sofa or bed to protect its occupant from being bitten by *konops,* a Greek word meaning mosquito. The sense of something —in this case a decorative fabric—on top of something else—a bed—was adopted by the French to describe an hors d'oeuvre consisting of a piece of bread or cracker over which a tasty topping has been spread.

canard—*Canard,* which was originally a French word for a duck, is now synonymous with *hoax.* Brewer's *Book of Phrase and Fable* reveals the following "fowl" story that caused the word *canard* to become a synonym for something that is a sham:

> Cornelissen, to try the gullibility of the public, reported in the papers that he had twenty ducks, one of which he cut up and threw to the nineteen, who devoured it greedily. He then cut up another, and then a third, and so on until nineteen were cut up; and as the nineteenth was gobbled up by the surviving duck, it followed that this one duck actually ate nineteen ducks—a wonderful proof of duck voracity.

This story apparently had the run of all the papers and provided a new meaning to the word *canard.*

Canard, in the parlance of continental (French) cuisine, refers to dishes made with duck.

candy ass (also **candy-ass** and **candy-assed**)/ **candy** / **candy man** / **candy kid** / **candy striper**—During the Watergate scandal of the 1970s, *candy ass* was used by President Nixon and his closest advisers and was recorded on those infamous tapes. Despite such august usage, *candy ass,* which is defined as a wimp, *milksop* (which see), sissy, or simply a weak person, has not achieved sweet success and is rarely heard today.

candy—a nickname for cocaine, hashish, or any barbiturate.

candy man—a man who sells drugs.

candy kid—a young man who is stylishly dressed; a showy person.

candy striper—one who performs volunteer work in a hospital as a nurse's aide and wears a distinctive stripe on his/her uniform.

carbohydrate(s) / carbo(s) / carbo-loading / carbonaut—*Carbohydrate,* which is also known as food starch, is a scientific term coined by Antoine Lavoisier. It combines *carbo,* a Latin word that means charcoal, and *hydrate,* from the Greek word *hydor,* meaning water.

The slang or shortened version of *carbohydrate(s)* is naturally *carbo(s).* Carbos are extremely important to athletes who are known to indulge in *carbo-loading,* the practice of eating large quantities of carbohydrates (often pastas) for several days leading up to a major athletic contest. In this way the *carbonaut* stores up reserves of glycogen, or animal starch, in the liver and muscles.

carrot / carrot top / carrot and stick—The carrot's root, in addition to being edible, is named after an ancient Greek word meaning a head, presumably because the reddish *carrot top* emerges slightly above the ground's surface (and explains why a redheaded person is called a carrot top).

One may easily speculate that the carrot's use in an incentive sense was popularized by a famous speech Winston Churchill (1874–1965) delivered on May 25, 1943, in which he said, "We shall continue to operate on the Italian donkey at both ends, with a carrot and with a stick." Others have traced the phrase *carrot and stick* to an even earlier use in a Humphrey Bogart film of the early 1940s.

The *carrot and stick* metaphor implies that you dangle some form of incentive, in this case a carrot, in front of a person while at the same time you prod him or her from behind with some additional stimulus, such as a stick or a threat of one kind or another.

cauliflower ear—Eatiomatically, a *cauliflower ear* is a descriptive slang name for a boxer's ear that has been badly deformed by repeated blows. The cauliflower, whose name literally means flowered cabbage, is a member of the mustard family.

caviar to the general—The "general" in this eatiom is not a military person at all, but refers instead to the general public, to whom caviar would be unknown in the time of Shakespeare, who popularized this phrase in *Hamlet*. It describes an idea, thought, or thing that the masses would not readily understand.

chazerai—Hebrew dietary laws derived from the Old Testament forbid observant Jews from consuming pork and pork by-products, and only permit the eating of animals that chew their cuds and that have cloven hooves, such as cattle and sheep. For this reason *chazerai,* a Yiddish word derived from the Hebrew word *khazer,* meaning pig, has developed the more general sense of something of little value or worthless—junk.

cheesecake / cheese, big / cheesecloth / cheesy / cheese-eater / cheesed off / cheese it / cheeseparing / cheese-head / cheese, the moon is made of green—*Cheesecake* is a slang expression for scantily clad beautiful women and pictures thereof. To describe briefly dressed men, there is *beefcake* (which see).

Credit for this colloquial morsel goes to cheesecake enthusiast Jim Kane of the *New York Journal.* Kane, a lover of the dessert cheesecake and pretty women, was assigned to take photos of celebrities returning by ocean liner to New York Harbor on a windy day in 1912. One of the celebrities, a beautiful young woman, was posing for Kane when a gust of wind lifted her dress, revealing her legs. Upon seeing them, Kane reportedly said, "Now, that's real cheesecake." His *cheesecake* remark was apparently a reference to the similarity between the color of the woman's leg and Kane's favorite dessert.

big cheese—derived from the Hindi word *chiz,* which means thing. A big *chiz,* therefore, is a big thing, and has come to mean an important person.

cheesecloth—an open-mesh cotton fabric originally used to wrap cheese. One of its current uses is in the polishing of cars.

cheesy—of or like cheese; having a cheesy aroma; inferior or cheap.

cheese-eater—an informer; rat; someone who betrays another.

cheesed off—British slang meaning disgusted.

cheese it—a warning cry to be silent, originally used by thieves to alert their cohorts that someone was coming. This idiom is derived from *cease it.*

cheeseparing—something of little value; stinginess; a skinflint who carefully shaves off the rind of the cheese instead of cutting it off.

cheesehead—a stupid person.

the moon is made of green cheese—an eatiom that can be traced back hundreds of years. New cheese, which looks quite a bit like the moon, is called green cheese.

cherry / cherry picker / cherry-top / cherry pie / cherry bomb / cherries, bowl of / cherry, Irish—The word *cherry* is derived from the Greek word *kerasia,* which has long been associated with Kerasos, in Asia Minor. It is also possible that Kerasos, a province of northeastern Turkey now called Giresun, was so named because of the abundance of cherry trees found there.

cherry—a virgin; a first offender; something that has not been used before, like a new car (or an old one that is in excellent condition).

cherry picker—a moveable boom that has a bucket attachment at the top large enough for a person. It is used to gain access to high places (such as telephone poles).

cherry-top—a police car, so called because of the red lights mounted on the roof.

cherry pie—something that is easy to obtain or achieve.

cherry bomb—a round red firecracker with dangerously high explosive capability.

bowl of cherries—something that is very good or pleasant.

Irish cherry—a carrot.

chestnut—A *chestnut* is eatiomatic for a tired or stale joke or anecdote that people are not too nuts about. Numerous authorities have traced this old-joke meaning to an 1816 play, *The Broken Sword,* by William Dimond. In this old *chestnut,* Captain Xavier spins an oft-told tale involving a cork tree. His friend, Pablo, corrects him by explaining that it was a chestnut and not a cork tree. Despite the captain's insistence that it was a cork tree, Pablo explains that he has heard the story dozens of times and it was, indeed a *chestnut.*

chestnuts out of the fire, pull one's—Aesop (620–560 B.C.) was a famous Greek slave and story teller, whose fables dramatized man's strengths and weaknesses, with people usually in the guise of animals. One of Aesop's masters was so charmed by the wisdom contained in his slave's tales that he freed him. It has been claimed that some of the stories credited to Aesop might actually have been written after his death. Both Plato and Socrates, it is said, heaped praise on this fabulous fabulist.

Two phrases come to us from the *chestnut* fable, a story about a monkey and a cat who were sitting in front of a fire, roasting chestnuts. In order to pull the chestnuts out of the roaring fire, the monkey used the cat's paw. In this way the cat's paw got burned while the monkey remained unharmed. To *pull one's chestnuts out of the fire* now means to save the day, or to rescue something/someone from a difficult situation.

The other side of this story provides us with the phrase *cat's-paw,* which explains Aesop's message from the viewpoint of the cat, the injured party in this fable. A cat's-paw has come to mean a person who, willingly or not, serves the purposes of another.

chew / chew out / chew someone's ear off / chew over / chew the fat / chew the rag / chew the scenery / chewed up—*Chew* evolved from the Old English word *ceowan,* meaning to bite or grind with the teeth. Chewing enables us to more easily swallow and digest our food.

chew—to reprimand.

chew out—to thoroughly bawl out someone; upbraid.

chew someone's ear off—to talk to someone at length; to talk incessantly.

chew over—to discuss; converse.

chew the fat—engage in friendly conversation.

chew the rag—same as *chew the fat.*

chew the scenery—to overact.

chewed up—to be thoroughly defeated.

chicken/chicken-livered/chickenhearted/chicken, spring/chicken out/chicken feed/chickie/chick/chicken shit / chicken-and-egg / chickens before they hatch, don't count your—There is some debate about which came first, the chicken or the chick. There are those who assume that *chicken* is the plural of *chick.* But chicken actually preceded chick, and its plural is chickens.

chicken—baloney, bunk, small tasks, cowardly. All of these meanings express the inconsequential or cowardly nature of chickens and chicks.

chicken-livered—cowardly.

chickenhearted—cowardly.

spring chicken—usually expressed in the negative: *he's/she's no spring chicken,* meaning a person is no longer young.

chicken out—to withdraw from a task or activity because of fear.

chicken feed—a small amount of money analogous to the feed given to chickens.

chickie—a warning to one's conspirators in order to prevent detection.

chick—a young woman (now considered sexist).

chicken shit—an inconsequential matter; pettiness; a lie; meaningless rules.

chicken-and-egg—a situation that is a dilemma because of the age-old question, Which came first, the chicken or the egg?

don't count your chickens before they hatch—
This idiom has its counterpart in most languages and can be traced to Aesop. His fable recounts the story of a woman who had a basket of eggs she was taking to the market, where she was planning to exchange them for a goose. In time, she figured, she would make enough from the goose to buy a cow. In her excitement she dropped the basket, breaking all her eggs.

chit—*Chit* is a word that means a bill for food or drink, or any receipt or voucher.

In addition to *chit* and *chintzy*, the word *cheetah*, for the fastest land animal, is also related to the Sanskrit root *citra*, something that is marked or spotted. The Hindi alteration of *citra*, *citth*, was first adopted by the English as *chitty* before it was shortened to *chit*. The cheetah is also brightly marked, as is *chintz*, a low-quality fabric whose name was altered to *chintzy*, meaning something of inferior worth; cheap; or someone who doesn't like to pay the *chit*.

chocolate / chocolate drop / chocolate box—Chocolate was the name of a drink popular with the Aztecs of Mexico, who were conquered by Cortés in 1521. The Aztec word for the chocolate drink that they made from the cocoa bean was *xocalatl,* which combined *xococ,* meaning bitter, and *atl,* meaning water. *Xococ* is also the origin of the word *cocoa.*

Xocalatl, according to chronicles of that period, was made by grinding cocoa seeds, whipping them in hot water, and flavoring the resulting concoction with vanilla. Cortés brought the beans back to Europe, where the Spaniards contributed to the development of modern-day chocolate by adding sugar. Later, in the eighteenth century, the English added milk and opened specialty houses where a sweetened form of *xocalatl,* which eventually was anglicized to *chocolate,* was served.

Cocoa beans were so highly prized that they were, at one time, used as a medium of exchange. To this day "beans" remains a slang term for money. The bean's monetary definition, however, is derived from the French word *bien,* meaning good, which was first used as a nickname for the English guinea coin of the 1840s.

A *chocolate box* is something that is excessively ornate, like the designs often found on a box of candy.

47

chops, lick one's / chops, flap one's / chops, down in the / chops, punch in the / chopsticks / chop-chop—
The first four of these "chop" eatioms are derived from an Anglo-Saxon root that means mouth or jaw. Therefore, to *lick one's chops* really means to salivate (drool) when confronted with, or in response to the smell of, well-prepared food. By the same token, to flap one's chops (gums or teeth) means to talk too much. While Americans might be *down in the mouth,* our British linguistic cousins would substitute *chops* for mouth, as in *down in the chops.*

The word *chopsticks,* for Chinese eating utensils, is not related to the above phrases. Instead, it is derived from the Chinese phrase *k'wai tse,* meaning the quick ones. "Chopsticks," played on a piano, is probably derived from this same Chinese source. The movement of the fingers in producing musical *chopsticks* is similar to those of the Chinese eating implements. *Chop-chop,* by the way, is derived from Pidgin English, and is undoubtedly related to *k'wai tse,* and means quickly.

chow / chow down / chow hall / chow hound—
Chow, which is an English slang word for food or

a mealtime, is, according to the *Oxford English Dictionary,* the name of an edible dog bred in China, also known as a *chow chow.* It came into English via the Pidgin (business) English used by Chinese merchants to communicate with their non-Chinese-speaking trading partners. It should be added that *chowchow* is also a Chinese word for an oriental relish.

chow down—to dine.

chow hall—see *mess hall.*

chow hound—an enthusiastic eater.

chowderhead—The term *chowderhead* has nothing to do with chowder soup. The inedible chowder element in this word is derived from the dialect word *chowterhead,* common in the Lancashire region of England, which was in turn derived from the Germanic word *jolterhead,* for someone who had received a jolt in the head. The anglicized version, *chowderhead,* means a stupid person, a blockhead.

chuck wagon—*Chuck,* meaning a cut of beef between the neck and shoulder blades, became a generic term for provisions in the American West. It was for this reason that the word *chuck* was mobilized to become *chuck wagon,* the meals on wheels of yesteryear that carried food to cowboys and other field workers when they happened to be too far out on the range to ride in for a meal.

clam at high tide, happy as a / clam up / clamshell / clam trap / clambake—*Happy as a clam at high tide* is an unusual animal metaphor because it is based on the humorous assumption that the clam has the same mental and emotional capacity as man, and further assumes that a clam should be happy when the tide is high because clams are only dug at low tide.

The word *clam* can be traced to the Old English word *claman,* meaning to grasp or fetter. *Clandestine,* meaning executed in secrecy, is also derived from the bivalve, and combines *clam,* meaning secretly, and *testinus,* meaning intestines. Because of the clam's tendency to close its shells for protection, the phrase *clam up* has come into use and means to be silent. A *clam* is also musician's slang for a wrong note. *Clamshell* and *clam trap* are slang eatioms for the mouth.

Clambake can be used to describe any number of kinds of parties, political meetings, or music sessions, but rarely one at which clams are actually baked.

cob, on (off) the / cob, rough as a—The name for the core (or cob) of the farmer's diet, corn, came to be used as an eatiom for the unsophisticated entertainment thought to be preferred by rural folks (see *corny*). While there isn't a kernel of truth in the idea that the farmer's taste in humor is unsophisticated, the perception remains that this is the case. In fact, the *corn* or *corny* sense has even spilled over to the core, or in this case the cob, of an ear of corn. *On the cob* and *off the cob* have, in turn, become synonymous with things that are considered corny. The word *cob,* of Scandinavian origin, has the basic sense of something rounded like a nut or corncob.

Rough as a cob describes a thing that is physically rough to the touch, or a person whose manner is rough. This idiom is derived from the fact that the cob, after it had been shed of its kernels, was—and is probably still—used in some parts as a primitive toilet paper.

cocktail—*Cocktail,* in addition to being a general term for mixed alcoholic beverages, has come also to mean an eclectic mixture of things including fruits, juices, seafoods, and even drugs.

In 1809, Washington Irving referred to ". . . those recondite beverages, cocktail, stonefence, and sherry cobbler." He was alluding to several mixed drinks, one of which, *cocktail,* became the generic name for all such beverages. The *cocktail* that Irving referred to was probably derived from a drink prepared by Antoine Peychard, a New Orleans druggist who mixed cognac and bitters and served the mixture in an eggcup. In French an eggcup is a *coquetier. Coquetier* was eventually anglicized to *cocktail.*

cold shoulder—In the days of chivalry, knights would travel the land slaying dragons and saving damsels in distress. These gallant men were generally welcomed warmly at the great palaces and castles along their way, and were refreshed with hot meals befitting their importance. In those days a traveler's status determined the size, quality, and even the temperature of his meal. The common traveler, for instance, when received at all, was not treated as cordially as those of high rank. For food, the commoner might get a shoulder of very lean mutton served cold. This kind of discourteous treatment has survived in the eatiom *cold shoulder,* which has come to mean a snub, disregard, or impoliteness toward someone.

company / **companion** / **pantry**—*Company* is another one of those ancient eatioms that have entered the realm of standard English words (see *precocious*). This friendly word combines the Latin words *cum* and *panis,* literally meaning *with bread,* but has come to convey the sense of those with whom we eat. Such people are *companions.* A *panetarius* was a baker in ancient Rome, and later the French called the place where he stored bread a *paneterie,* a word that was eventually anglicized to *pantry.* Today, a pantry is more generally a closet where groceries, household goods, and other provisions are stored.

cook / **cook up** / **cook with gas** / **cookout** / **cook the books** / **cooked** / **cooker, pressure**—The ancient Romans did not *cook with gas,* but the Latin word for *cook, cocus,* has undergone little change in two thousand years.

cook up—to fabricate; to make up a story, create an alibi.

cook with gas—to be knowledgeable; to do the correct thing; to be hip (jazz use). When gas ranges first came into use, they provided housewives and professional cooks with an efficient and uniform heat source for cooking. *Cooking with gas,* therefore, had a very positive connotation.

cookout—a meal cooked out of doors on a backyard grill (see *barbecue*).

cook the books—to knowingly falsify records, especially financial accounts.

cooked—ruined; destroyed.

pressure cooker—a condition or place that causes great mental stress.

cookie / cookie jar, have one's hand in the / cookies, spill one's / cookie crumbles, that's the way the / cookie-cutter—The cookie, in addition to being a small cake, has become eatiomatic for a dear, a sweetheart, or an alluring young woman. Cookie is also used to describe a person who is singled out for special respect, such as a smart or tough cookie. Cookie is derived from *koekje,* the diminutive of the Dutch word *koek,* meaning a cake.

to have one's hand in the cookie jar—to take advantage of one's position or status by asking for and getting bribes.

to spill one's cookies—to vomit.

that's the way the cookie crumbles—that's fate; the way things happen (similar to *that's the way the ball bounces*).

cookie-cutter—an adjective used to describe something that lacks originality and is hackneyed or conventional.

cordon bleu chef—At horse, dog, and state farm shows, the best animals (and in the case of horse shows, the best horse and rider) are awarded a blue ribbon, a classic symbol of supremacy. High honor as represented by the color blue can be traced back to the ancient Greeks and Romans, whose gods and goddesses, it was thought, lived in the heavens beyond the blue sky. As a result of this heavenly connection, the color blue has been reserved throughout history for honors of the greatest distinction. The Knights of Saint Esprit (Holy Ghost), the highest order of French chivalry, was established during the time of the Bourbon kings (1589–1792). Each of these knights wore a medallion attached to a *cordon bleu* (blue ribbon). England's highest honor of knighthood, the Order of the Garter, established by King Edward III about 1348, also utilized a blue ribbon.

The members of the French Knights of Saint Esprit had an exclusive dining club where fine gourmet dinners were served. The blue ribbon, symbolic of the order, was transferred to the food and chefs of the dining club, and the phrase *cordon bleu* took on the meaning of excellence in food preparation.

The phrases *cordon bleu* and *blue ribbon* have also come to be applied to someone who has achieved great distinction in any field.

corn-fed / **corny** / **corn** / **cornball**—Traveling vaudeville actors were acutely aware of the differing tastes of country and city audiences. Since country people were surrounded by corn, they were described as *corn-fed* because the farmers' diet consisted largely of that staple. Later, *corn-fed* was used to describe the unsubtle humor preferred by farmers. Finally, *corn-fed* was shortened to *corny,* which Webster describes as unsophisticated, old-fashioned, trite, banal, and sentimental; and a *cornball* is someone who likes *corn* or *corny* entertainment.

crabby / crab / crabwise / crab, catch a—The *lemon* (which see) is not the only food that has been eatiomatically personified to describe people who are grouchy or ill-natured. *Crabby,* also meaning grumpy and irritable, has two possible origins. Some authorities believe that the negative connotation of *crabby* or *crab* originates with the sour taste of a smallish member of the apple family, the crabapple. But there are those who are equally certain that it's from the tendency of the shellfish crab to reside in the crevices of rocks, a habit that makes it appear to man as morose or peevish. *Crabwise* describes a person who walks sideways as a crab does, or as a person might do when traversing a row of seats in a theater.

Catch a crab is a term used in collegiate rowing to describe the failure to dip one's oar in the water and thereby miss the stroke, and/or failing to lift the oar from the water. In either case this can bring about a catastrophe for the crew. The expression arose, no doubt, from a rower's jocular excuse after missing a stroke, that he *caught (hit) a crab.*

cracker/crackers/cracker factory/cracker barrel/ crackerjack—*Cracker* has several separate senses, all of which can be traced to the Old English word *cracian,* meaning to resound. *Cracker* is related to *crack* and *craze* as well.

cracker—a thin and very crisp biscuit that makes a cracking noise when broken in half; a rolled paper favor used at children's parties that makes a loud cracking or snapping sound (also called a snapper); a boaster or braggart; someone who cracks jokes; a Georgia cracker. *Cracker* also designates a special buggy whip with a piece of leather at the end that makes a cracking sound; formerly used by Georgia coastal dwellers, it is suggested as the source of the phrase *Georgia cracker.*

crackers—a chiefly British word that means crazy. Both *crackers* and *crazy* are derived from the older sense of to craze or crush. *Crackers* became a metaphor for someone who was mentally impaired, not whole or complete.

cracker factory—an insane asylum.

cracker barrel—a metaphor for rural old-fashioned philosophy. It was the practice of small-town folks to gather around the traditional *cracker barrel* in the typical country store where they would dispense a special brand of homespun wisdom.

crackerjack—one who is wonderful, remarkable, or superior in a particular activity. This superlative combines *crack-*, as in a crack or expert shot with a rifle, and *-jack,* a common nickname used for a man when his real name is unknown. The term was further popularized in the late nineteenth century when Cracker Jack was used as a trade name by the firm F. W. Rueckheims and Brother for a mixture of popcorn, peanuts, and a molasses syrup.

cream of the crop / cream rises to the top / cream / cream puff—For the most part, the roots of the word *cream* have risen to the top in an affirmative way. The positive direction of its roots, for example, is observed in the ancient Greek word *krisma,* an anointing or an oil used for that purpose. *Khristos*, the past participle of the verb *khrein,* to anoint, means the anointed one. Khristos became the name by which Jesus Christ was known.

cream of the crop—the best; the preferred choice.

cream rises to the top—a metaphor that suggests that the best person or thing usually surpasses all others.

cream—This word has a range of meanings including to do something exceedingly well; to have spectacular success on an exam; the best of any classification; something that is easy or pleasant; to defeat easily.

cream puff—ranges in meaning from a weak ineffectual person to something, such as an automobile made ready for sale, that has been maintained in excellent condition.

creole—In the sixteenth century, after the Spanish had colonized the West Indies, they used the word *criollo* to distinguish those people born in the islands of Spanish and other European families from European immigrants, Negroes, or Indians who lived in or were native to the New World. *Criollo* is derived from the Latin word *creare*, meaning to create. Originally, *criollo,* which is now spelled *creole,* referred to those who were newly "created" in that part of the Spanish Empire.

In the United States, *creole* first described those descendants of the early French, Spanish, and Portuguese settlers who lived in the Gulf states, primarily Louisiana. *Creole* is also used to describe people of mixed black and European ancestry. *Creole* dishes consist of spicy chili sauces, tomatoes, peppers, onions, celery, and other seasonings and are generally served with rice.

crispy—The word *crispy* is derived from the Latin word *crispus,* meaning the curling of hair.

The Romans used the curlicue appearance of hair curls as a metaphor for the appearance of some foods, such as bacon, that curl when fried. Such foods that were called *crispy* were also very fragile, providing another meaning: easily breakable. Crisp foods, as opposed to soggy ones, were generally deemed to be fresh, and thus *crispy* came to mean fresh. *Brisk* and *lively* probably stem from the fresh sense as well.

The "clean-cut" connotation probably resulted from the original sense of the Latin *crispus,* because hair, when arranged with tight curls, is very neat and provides a clean-cut appearance.

crumb (crum) / crumb-bun / crumb joint / crumby (crummy)—We have only to look at the *crumb*'s ancestry to discover how its pejorative offsprings went wrong. *Crumb,* you see, is derived from the Germanic word *krume,* a heap of earth.

>   **crumb (crum)**—a dirty, messy, despicable person; one who cannot be trusted; one who is objectionable or insignificant.

>   **crumb-bun**—a worthless person.

>   **crumb joint**—a cheap hotel; flophouse.

>   **crumby (crummy)**—run-down; dirty; seedy.

cucumber, as cool as a—One who is *as cool as a cucumber* is unflappable, placid, serene. It is likely that since *cucumbers* were at one time available only in the hot months of the year and were served cold, they became symbolic of something cool to eat as opposed to foods generally served hot. Because of its green color, *cucumber* has become one of the many vegetable-slang synonyms for the dollar.

Dead Sea fruit—The Dead Sea is a salt lake nestled between the borders of Jordan and Israel and is so named because of its 26 percent salt content, which makes it virtually impossible for the water to support life.

Apple and orange trees grow on the shores of this lake, and although the fruits of these trees look very appetizing, they are bitter tasting, due to their absorption of salt and minerals. *Dead Sea fruit,* then, has come to mean anything that appears to be beautiful or promising, but turns out to be a big disappointment.

delly (dellie, deli) counter / delly food—The *Oxford English Dictionary* attributes *delicatessen* to a German word defined as delicacies for the table. *Delicatessen* combines the German elements *delicat-* and *-essen,* which together literally mean to eat delicacies. Delicate, itself, is derived from the

Latin word *delicere,* to turn aside by trickery or seduction.

desserts / deserts, just—*Just deserts* first appeared in English in 1380 A.D., in Chaucer's translation of *The Consolation of Philosophy* by Boethius. The phrase is derived from the Old French word *deserte,* which is the past participle of *deservir,* meaning to be deserving or worthy. The first word in the phrase, *just,* means fair, and when linked with *deserts,* means fair reward, and can indicate both prize or punishment.

Dessert, on the other hand, is a dinner course served at the end of a meal. *Dessert* is derived from the Old French word *desservir,* which literally means to remove that which has already been served.

dish (cup) of tea, not my / dish / dish it out / dish the dirt / dishy—*Dish* can be traced back to the Latin word *discus,* meaning a dish, but was derived from the even older Greek word *diskos,* a platter or quoit (a ring of rope or metal thrown at an upright peg for amusement). *Tea,* incidentally, is an anglicized form of the Malaysian word *teh,* which in turn can be traced to the Chinese word *cha,* a specific brand of rolled tea.

not my dish (cup) of tea—to dislike something.

dish—a beautiful, pretty, or alluring woman (now considered sexist).

dish it out—to issue abuse, news, talk, or gossip.

dish the dirt—to gossip.

dishy—the British rendition of the *dish* eatiom, above.

doughboy / dough / doughnuts, dollars to / doughball / doughfoot / doughhead / doughnut—The first recorded use of *doughboy* to describe a U.S. infantry soldier was by Gen. George Armstrong Custer in 1867.

Infantrymen were first called *doughboys* during the Civil War, one theory goes, because the buttons on their uniforms looked like doughboys (globs of dough). Others trace the *doughboy* idiom to the Mexican War, when soldiers lived in adobe huts and were called adobe boys, dobe boys, and finally doughboys.

dough—money (see *bread*).

dollars to doughnuts—In 1890, the expression *dollars to doughnuts* replaced dollars to buttons and other such expressions used to describe something that was almost a certainty.

doughball—an uninteresting or dull person.

doughfoot—an infantry soldier.

doughhead—a stupid person.

doughnut—a car tire.

duck soup / ducky / duck walk / ducktail / duck's ass —When something is extremely easy we say that it is *duck soup,* an extension of the expression *sitting duck,* which describes the hunter's good fortune when he sees a duck resting on the water in range of his rifle. *Duck soup* has developed the sense of something very easy, as well as a person easy to cheat, or a cinch.

ducky—excellent, fine, wonderful. The British use it as a term of familiar address or affection; someone who is darling or cute.

duck walk—a walk like that of a duck.

ducktail / duck's ass—a haircut in which the back of the hair is cut in similar fashion to the natural shape of a duck's tail feathers.

egg / egg on / egg sucker / eggs, don't teach your grandmother to suck / egg money / egg, goose / egg, lay an / egg, bad / egg, good / egg, hard-boiled / egg, tough / egghead / egg in your beer / egg on one's face / eggs in one basket, put all one's / eggs, walk on / eggbeater / eggs is eggs, as sure as / egg, nest / eggs of Nuremberg / eggs to apples / eggs, like as two / eggs for my money, I got / eggs, scrambled / ham-and-egger / eggs, you can't make an omelet without breaking—The ancient Norse word *egg* probably has some relationship to the Greek and Latin words for the *egg, oion* and *ovum,* respectively.

egg on—to encourage or urge, derived from a medieval Germanic word that literally means to put an egg on edge.

egg sucker—a person who seeks promotion by flattery rather than hard work. This is an apparent reference to the tendency of certain animals, such as the weasel, to suck the contents of bird's eggs.

don't teach your grandmother to suck eggs—to presume that you can teach an older person new tricks, particularly someone with the experience and wisdom of a grandmother.

egg money—small sums of money that a person might earn from the sale of eggs, butter, and other incidental farm produce.

goose egg—For centuries the egg has been symbolic of zero, apparently because of its similarity to the Arabic numeral. A *goose egg* is used in sports patois to indicate a score of zero for a person or team. The word *love* in tennis, which also represents no score for a contestant, is considered by many to be derived from the French term *l'oeuf,* the egg.

lay an egg—to tell a joke that doesn't go over; to strike out; to fail.

rotten or bad egg—a thoroughly bad or rotten person, an obvious reference to the foul smell and taste of an egg that has spoiled.

good egg—a good person.

hard-boiled egg—someone who is unsentimental; tough; also a stingy person (colloquial sense from the 1930s).

tough egg—same sense as the hard-boiled variety.

egghead—an intellectual or artsy person. Most sources feel that this term was first applied to Adlai Stevenson and his intellectual supporters during the 1952 presidential election campaign. Perhaps the intellectual sense of this eatiom stems from the egglike appearance of bald-headed men, which sometimes makes them appear brainier than those with a full head of hair.

egg in your beer—a nineteenth-century eatiom directed at someone who requests a luxury far beyond what is reasonable—usually preceded by "Whataya want . . . ?"

egg on your face—to be embarrassed or humiliated because of some action that is unwise or foolish.

put all one's eggs in one basket—to gamble one's money, energies, and dreams on the success of a single investment, effort, or event. This phrase is based on the loss suffered when a basket filled with one's total egg production is stolen or falls to the ground. The extent of such a loss can be lessened by carrying the eggs in more than one basket or diversifying investments so that they are not concentrated in one place.

walk on eggs—to walk or act very carefully or discreetly.

eggbeater—a slang synonym for a helicopter.

as sure as eggs is eggs—something certain. There is no mistaking eggs, but this eatiom, paradoxically, has nothing to do with eggs. In fact, the use of eggs in this case was a distortion of the equation $X is$ (*equals*) $X,$ which in mathematical terms is a sure thing.

nest egg—money set aside for retirement, a child's education, or for any special goal. The *nest egg,* usually made of porcelain, was—and probably still is—placed in a chicken's nest to induce her to lay eggs. When someone begins to save money for a special occasion, the pool of money, once established, induces that person to continue saving.

eggs of Nuremberg—In the sixteenth century, watches were first made in Nuremberg, Germany, and shaped like eggs; they soon became known as *eggs of Nuremberg*.

eggs to apples—from first to last. Today, all of the courses in an elaborate meal might be described as from soup to nuts. The ancient Romans, however, began their feasts with eggs and polished them off with apples.

like as two eggs—identical—usually used to describe twins who look alike.

I got eggs for my money—to give valuable goods or money and receive something as relatively worthless as eggs in return.

scrambled eggs—Since World War II, this slang expression has referred to the braiding that is worn on the hat brims of hotshot military senior officers.

ham-and-egger—a person who plods along without much ambition or success; a club fighter (boxer) who enters bouts merely for food money; a person in show business who never achieves financial or artistic success.

you can't make an omelet without breaking eggs—The word *omelet* is derived from the Latin word *lamina* (the source of *laminate*) and *lame,* originally a thin metal plate used as part of a suit of armor. Omelets were apparently fried on thin metal plates by the ancients. This eatiom, which essentially means to do something bad for the greater good, is attributed to Russian revolutionary leader Lenin who, of course, broke many an egg in his time.

enchilada, big / enchilada, whole—A *big enchilada* is Spanish-American eatiom inspired by Mexican cookery and it means the big boss; the chief or main person. The *whole enchilada* (*enchilada*'s middle name is chili) is a related eatiom meaning the entirety of any particular thing.

F

farrago—*Farrago* has come to mean a mixture of different things, a medley, and is taken directly from a Latin word of the same spelling, meaning a mixture of cattle fodder.

fat's in the fire / fat chance / fat of the land / fat, chew the / fathead / fat cat / fat farm—

fat's in the fire—an irreversible action or chain of events. Every cook knows that when the fat falls into the fire it causes a sudden flare-up and a rapid end to the fat.

fat chance—a very small chance. This is an ironic construction based upon the idiom *a slim chance,* which is synonymous with a fat chance.

fat of the land—the best of anything that can be obtained.

chew the fat—talk in an easy manner.

fathead—an incompetent or stupid person.

fat cat—someone who provides funds for political campaigns; a person who has wealth, fame, and many luxuries.

fat farm—a place where people go to lose weight.

feed / feed, off one's / feedbag / feedbag, put on the / feed one's face / feedback / fed up / feed a line / feed the kitty—The word *feed* is akin to the Anglo-Saxon words *foda, food,* and *fodor,* food for animals (fodder).

feed—a very lavish meal.

off one's feed—depressed or sad. Stems from the behavior of an animal that refuses to eat.

feedbag—meal or dinner. Horses are often served from a canvas or leather bag full of oats or other grains.

put on the feedbag—to dine.

feed one's face—eat.

feedback—response to an action.

fed up—bored or disgusted.

feed a line—conversation engaged in by a person to impress or seduce another person.

feed the kitty—to contribute to a common cause.

fig, don't care a/fig, in full—In the case of the eatiom *don't care a fig,* the fig was derived from the Italian word *fico,* meaning the snap of a finger. The phrase, like the snapping gesture, has come to symbolize something that is worthless; a trifling amount. The other fig-related phrase, *in full fig,* can be traced to the German word, *fegen,* which means to spruce up or clean and polish.

fig, sign of the—The *sign of the fig,* which can be traced back to the ancient Greeks, is a gesture of contempt that is also considered obscene. Made by thrusting the thumb between the first and second digits of the hand, this gesture was first used by *sycophants* (which see) to point out suspected fig smugglers.

Prior to man's developing the ability to communicate vocally, the hands played a major role in conveying his thoughts and emotions.

fish / fishy / fish-wrapper / fish tale / fishbowl / fish eggs / fishhooks / fish or cut bait / fish story / fish, April / fish, fine kettle of / fish stare / fish eater / fish, poor / fish, queer / fish, big / fish to fry, bigger / fish, cold / fish in a rain barrel, like shooting / fish, tin / fish out of water / fish in troubled waters—

fish—a person who is easily taken advantage of; a sucker; a weak opponent in sports; a dollar; to seek information; to ask for a compliment.

fishy—something dishonest or unethical.

fish-wrapper—a newspaper.

fish tale—an alibi or excuse.

fishbowl—a jail.

fish eggs—tapioca pudding.

fishhooks—fingers.

fish or cut bait—to demand or request that someone perform successfully or stop and give someone else a chance to do so.

fish story—see *fish tale*.

April fish—an April fool.

fine kettle of fish—a mess, analogous to a pot or kettle filled with fish.

fish stare—a description of a person staring ahead blankly without blinking, like the eyes of a fish.

fish eater—a Roman Catholic.

poor fish—a person who is victimized by conditions beyond his or her control.

queer fish—a strange or weird person.

big fish—a big shot; an important person.

bigger fish to fry—said of one who has more important things to do.

cold fish—someone who lacks personal warmth.

like shooting fish in a rain barrel—something that is very easy to do.

tin fish—a torpedo.

fish out of water—a person out of his or her normal environment.

fish in troubled waters—to take advantage of troubled conditions for personal gain.

food, angel / food, bunny / food, fast / food, junk / food, soul/foodaholic/fodder/foster—Food can be traced to *foda,* an Anglo-Saxon word meaning food that is akin to fodder (see *feed*) meaning animal food. Both words are akin to and influenced by the Latin word *pascere,* to feed. As a result of the continual change in spelling and pronunciation that words often undergo throughout history, along with the consonant shift, *pascere* was transformed into *food* and *foster.*

angel food—the preaching that often follows a free meal at Salvation Army and other Christian mission headquarters.

bunny food—lettuce or salad, and raw vegetables.

fast food—foods prepared quickly and in large quantities in specialty restaurants and restaurant chains.

junk food—a food that is high in calories but low in nourishment.

soul food—traditional black food usually served in the southern states, consisting of fried chicken, chitterlings, kale, turnip greens, pigs' knuckles, corn bread, and the like.

foodaholic—someone who habitually overeats.

fodder—a bulk food served to livestock. Soldiers sent to war become *cannon fodder* (the targets of guns).

foster—to nourish or to rear with food; to nourish the mind with ideas.

fork / fork over (out) (up) / fork you—The word *fork* was derived from the Latin word *furcatus,* a fork-shaped farm utensil. Before the fork was miniaturized for use at the dining table, it was a two-tined (pronged) farm tool used for pitching hay, produce, and farm refuse. *Fork over* (*out*) (*up*) means to pay over, while the *fork* in *fork you* is a euphemism for the "f" word.

free lunch—The *free lunch* was a nineteenth-century promotion by western saloonkeepers to induce their customers to buy drinks. This practice survives in many bars that today still serve free hot and cold hors d'oeuvres to their drinking patrons.

Occasionally, a bar's proprietor would find it necessary to remind a customer that his consumption of the free buffet exceeded the value of his alcoholic purchases. In such cases he would undoubtedly advise the offending freeloader that "There is no *free lunch* at this establishment!" In other words, you don't get something for nothing.

fritter/fritter away time—*Fritters* can be a batter that is either panfried like a pancake or deep-fat fried and can also consist of bits of meat, fish, fruit, or vegetables that have been dipped in a batter, dried, and deep-fat fried. The word *fritter* is derived from the Latin word *frigere,* meaning to fry. But sometimes people *fritter away time,* or waste time, which has nothing to do with the edible fritters first mentioned. This wasteful kind of *fritter* is derived from the Latin word *frictura,* meaning a fragment.

fruit / fruitcake / fruit salad / vegetable / fruit, forbidden—

> **fruit**—a disparaging term for a homosexual; also an eccentric person. *Fruit* is derived from the Latin word *frutus,* meaning enjoyment, profit, something accomplished or attained.

> **fruitcake**—an insane or eccentric person; an oddball (because of the numerous nuts in such a cake); a derogatory term for a homosexual male.

> **fruit salad**—a slang eatiom for the colorful ribbons and badges worn by armed forces personnel.

> **vegetable**—a person who is mentally or physically impaired and not able to respond in a normal human way; one who is inactive, dull, inert.

> **forbidden fruit**—fruit from the tree of knowledge of good and evil that Adam and Eve tasted despite God's restriction; any morally wrong or illegal pleasure, especially of the sexual kind.

fry / fry, small / frying pan into the fire, out of the
—The use of the term *small fry* is derived from

the medieval English word *frie,* which means spawn. Fry is also used as a synonym for young animals, as well as children. It is not related, however, to the Latin verb *frigere,* which has spawned the following eatioms.

fry—to burn (die) in the electric chair; to chastise someone as exemplified by the Friar's Club, which regularly roasts its featured guests.

out of the frying pan into the fire—to go from bad to worse.

fudge—Fudge, best known as the soft candy made of chocolate, has also come to mean nonsense or foolish talk. Several sources trace *fudge* to the Gaelic and Welsh words *ffug,* meaning deception or pretense. A more interesting, but possibly fanciful origin was found in a pamphlet discovered by the father of English Prime Minister Benjamin Disraeli (1804–1881). In this version, Fudge, a merchant sea captain, was famous for losing his cargoes and then telling a pack of lies to explain how they were lost. He became known as Lying Fudge, and according to this rendition *fudge* came to mean cheat.

$$\boxed{\text{G}}$$

garnish—Garnishes, those special touches, enhance the appearance, taste, and overall enjoyment of food, as every great cook and gourmet knows.

Garnish is derived from an Old French word that meant to take warning. It was later used to describe the arms worn by soldiers and, still later, something ornamental applied to the armor itself. From this last sense garnish came to define the decorating or adorning of food or just about anything else.

ginger / ginger up / gingery / gingerly / gingerbread
—*Zingiber officinale,* the scientific name for *ginger,* is a plant native to East India, but is now grown in most tropical countries.

ginger—an ingredient that enlivens a performance (as in "the dancer had plenty of *ginger* in her performance").

84

ginger up—to spice up a performance.

gingery—something that is lively or spicy.

gingerly—the antonym of *gingery* means to do something very carefully, cautiously, or warily. It should come as no surprise, therefore, to discover that the *ginger* eatioms above bear no relationship to *gingerly*. *Gingerly*, instead, is derived, via Old French, from the Latin word *genitus*, a person who is wellborn, gracious, and attractive, and not given to awkward or hasty movements.

gingerbread—a cake, often made into decorative shapes, flavored with ginger and molasses. It has achieved eatiomatic stardom as something gaudily ornamented, and is often used to describe Victorian architecture. This special use of *gingerbread* is derived from the highly decorated gingerbread houses.

glop/gorp/gorp gobblers—

glop—a messy mixture of food; anything done sloppily.

gorp—an assortment consisting of nuts, seeds, dried fruits, and raisins. While *gorp* may be a variation of *glop,* there is another theory that suggests that *gorp* could be an acronym for **G**ood **O**ld **R**aisins and **P**eanuts. *Gorp* can also mean to eat without restraint. Because of its high energy potential, *gorp* is a favorite supplement for hikers and mountain climbers, who are also called *gorp gobblers.*

goose, cook your / goose egg / goose / goose someone (something) / goose hangs high / goose that laid the golden egg, kill the / goose bumps (flesh) / goose-drownder / goose, loose as a / goose step—A legend that can be traced back to the sixteenth century states that King Eric of Sweden had come to an enemy town with the intention of besieging it. This town's burghers, in a show of contempt for the king and his small band of men, hung a goose from a town tower and then sent a message to King Eric that in effect asked, "What do you want?" "To cook your goose," came the king's reply, whereupon the Swedes set fire to the town, cooking the goose in the process. This eatiom currently means to destroy one's chances or hopes.

goose egg—See *egg* entries.

goose—to pinch someone; a pinch in the buttocks, presumably because of the penchant of geese to do the same.

goose someone (something)—to hurry someone or something along; to accelerate a car or someone.

goose hangs high—an old expression that means that everything is okay or looking up. Some experts speculate that this eatiom is a variation of the *goose honks high*. Geese are said to fly at higher altitudes in good weather.

kill the goose that laid the golden egg—to act greedily and lose a steady source of income as a result. This phrase is derived from the fable in which a farmer who owned a goose that laid golden eggs killed the goose in order to obtain the eggs much faster. The result, of course, was that he cut off his steady source of golden eggs.

goose bumps (flesh)—small bumps on the skin caused by cold, fear, or excitement.

goose-drownder—a very heavy downpour.

loose as a goose—very easy; relaxed. (A trip to most parks where geese have taken up residence will convince you that geese have loose bowels.)

goose step—a military marching step like that of a goose.

goulash—Our word *goulash* is derived from the Hungarian word *gulyashes,* herdsman's meat, but was shortened to *gulyas* before it was anglicized to *goulash.* That these various stews are often made with leftovers and look like a mess when served suggests why goulash has become synonymous with a potpourri.

grapevine / grapefruit league / grape / grape, belt the / grape, Irish—*Grape* is derived from the Frankish word *grappa,* a hook. Grapes were so named because of the hooked shape of a bunch of grapes. *Grapple* is related to *grappa* by way of *grapnel,* a hook-shaped tool used for grasping and holding things.

grapevine—a vine that holds grapes. Because of the vine's tendency to send shoots out in all directions, gossip is said to be communicated through a grapevine of sources.

grapefruit league—a series of preseason baseball games played by major league baseball teams in the South's Citrus Belt.

grape—wine.

belt the grape—drink to excess.

Irish grapes—potatoes.

gravy / gravy train / gravy boat—*Gravy* was influenced by the Latin word *granata,* something grained. Gravy has historically been thickened with grains of flour.

gravy—money or profit easily or unexpectedly obtained; money dishonestly acquired; an unexpected benefit.

gravy train—a job that requires little or no work.

gravy boat—same as *gravy train;* also a boat-shaped bowl from which gravy is poured.

grease / grease pit / greasy spoon—*Crassus,* the Latin word from which the English word *grease* is derived, meant thick, fat, gross, and was probably prompted by animal fat as well. Undesirable *grease* stimulated these additional eatioms: *grease pit* and *greasy spoon* (see *spoon*), both meaning a cheap diner, lunchroom, or other restaurant where sanitation is poor.

gridiron / griddle cake / gridlock—*Gridiron* is derived from the Middle English words *gridirne* and *gredil,* metal grates. From this same source came *griddle* and *griddle cake* (see *pancakes* and *hot cakes*).

Gridirons were used for cooking meats and other foods over an open fire. These rectangular cooking devices with their parallel crossbars looked very much like miniature football fields. William and Mary Morris attributed the use of *gridiron* to describe a football field to a *Boston Herald* article of 1897. But in 1896 a story connecting football and the gridiron appeared in a *London Daily News* article.

Gridlock describes heavy traffic, or a condition in which there is little movement, such as a financial *gridlock* brought about by a bad economy.

grit / gritty / grit, clear—*Grit* has been used as a synonym for stamina, fortitude, or just plain guts since the late eighteenth century. During the Civil War Union writers described federal troops as having *clear grit.*

Grit is derived from an Old English word that was defined as granules of sand or other abrasive material. *Grits,* also referred to as hominy grits, are coarsely ground bleached corn commonly eaten in southern states as a breakfast cereal. *Hominy* is an anglicized version of a word used by the aboriginals of Virginia, who first prepared corn in this way.

Several authorities attribute the plucky sense of *grit* to the fact that chickens are known to put pebbles or sand in their craws to assist in grinding up their feed. A gamecock without sufficient sand or pebbles in its crop to grind its food would likely be underfed and, therefore, ill equipped to win in the arena.

grocery / groceries / groceries, bring home the— *Grocery* is derived from the Latin word *grossus,* meaning big or fat (the source for the word *gross*). The French version, *grossier,* came to define a vendor who sells in gross, bulk, or wholesale, and led to the English word *grocer.*

groceries—a meal or meals; any very important result or success (*bring home the groceries*); to earn money; to succeed (see *bacon, bring home the*).

grub / grub slinger / grubstake—*Grub* is derived from an old Germanic word that means to dig. One of the most important things that people have *grubbed* for throughout the ages has been the edible roots of plants, and this explains why *grub* has come to mean to eat, or simply *vittles* (which see). By the same token, a *grub slinger* is a slang term for a cook.

A *grubstake* is currently defined as money or other support, such as food and equipment, provided to a person or persons in order to start a new undertaking. The eatiom *grubstake* was dug up during the great American gold rush of the nineteenth century, when it pertained to a practice whereby a wealthy man, a *grubstaker*, would advance food and equipment, or a sum of money to purchase same, in return for a share of the prospector's gold.

ham actor / hamfat—Many etymologists insist that *ham* is simply a shortened, but breathy, version of *amateur*. This would explain the use of *ham* as a nickname for amateur radio enthusiasts. Next is the *hamfat* theory, which proposes that the term *ham* comes from a popular nineteenth-century song, "The Hamfat Man." This song described the life of second-rate actors. *Hamfat* was commonly used by actors of that period to remove greasepaint makeup.

Finally, etymologist Rosie Boycott suggests that *ham* comes from the nickname of Hamish McCollough (1835–1885), who toured the American Midwest with his acting troupe. According to Boycott's interesting theory, this group became known as Ham's actors, and ultimately *ham actors*. They were also known for their weak acting performance and, therefore, *ham actor* took on its current meaning of an actor who exaggerates or overacts.

hardtack—*Hardtack,* a hard, saltless, unleavened *biscuit* (which see) or bread made in large wafers, was used as army and navy rations before the advent of refrigeration. Hardtack's great advantage was that it would last longer and take up less space in the hold of a ship or the bed of a wagon than the leavened variety. The *hard-* part of this word is self-explanatory, merely an indication of its durability. The origin of *-tack,* however, a word meaning foodstuff, is unknown.

hash / hash, settle one's / hash of, make / hash over / rehash / hash out—*Hash* can be traced to the medieval French word *hacher,* meaning to chop up. *Hacher* was also defined as an ax, and the diminutive of *hacher, hachette,* eventually was anglicized to hatchet, a small ax.

hash—a dish of diced or chopped meat and often vegetables. *Hash* also has the colloquial sense of *hodgepodge* (which see), muddle, or mess.

settle one's hash—to get rid of; become angered at; subdue.

to make hash of—to bungle; botch.

94

hash over—to bring up again; to settle or re-solve.

rehash—to rediscuss.

hash out—to settle or resolve by lengthy dis-cussions.

It should be mentioned here that *hash* is also a shortened variant of *hashish,* the name of a drug made from the leaves of the Indian hemp. This variety of *hash* is chewed or smoked for its nar-cotic effect.

herring, red—When a herring is smoked, it turns a red color and becomes known as *red herring.* Prior to being smoked it is usually dried and salted, which not only imparts a special flavor but cures (preserves) the fish as well. Dog trainers use the *red herring* to teach their dogs to follow a scent by trailing it over the ground. Prior to the use of *red herrings,* dead cats and foxes were used for this purpose.

Pranksters discovered that tracking dogs could be diverted by dragging this smoked variety of fish over a fox trail, a trick that would surely ruin the hunt. Escaped prisoners were also aware that the *red herring* was helpful in throwing hounds off their scent.

high muckymuck (also **high muckamuck**)—This idiom can be traced to the North American Chinook Indian phrase *hiu macamac,* which translates into English as "plenty of food." A person who ate well in that culture was a very important person.

hodgepodge—A *hodgepodge* has come to mean a conglomeration, mess, or miscellany. It was originally derived from the medieval French phrase *hocier pot,* literally meaning a shake pot. This early French version was used to describe a conglomeration, probably of leftovers, that was placed in a stew pot for the next meal. The anglicized *hodgepodge* has essentially lost its connection with food in favor of its heterogeneous sense.

hog, high on the—Eating *high on the hog* is a comical way of saying eating well or sumptuously. This eatiom expresses what every farmer and butcher knows, that the best cuts of the hog are located on the upper parts of the animal. The word *hog* is probably of Celtic origin and, because of the hog's gluttonous ways, it has become a metaphor for a selfish or greedy person.

hog, whole—Going *whole hog* has nothing to do with food, but is defined as to go all out or to spend or bet all the money one has. This slang eatiom can be traced to seventeenth-century England, when a shilling was called a hog. It is also recorded that there was an Irish coin, as well as one from Bermuda, that had a hog embossed on it.

honeymoon / honey / honey wagon / honey barge/ honey bucket / honey man / honeycakes—Our efforts to trace the origin of *honeymoon,* that sweet period of new marital bliss, take us back to Teutonic societies of the Middle Ages when the first month after the wedding was called the Germanic equivalent of the honey month. The *honey* element in this word is attributed to the custom of drinking honey wine during this month.

While the *honeymoon* was originally the month after marriage, it has come to mean the vacation or holiday taken by newlyweds immediately after the wedding. *Honeymoon* is also used, idiomatically, to describe that period after an election when the victorious candidates or parties experience a period of agreement.

honey—a sweetheart; a terrific person; a very decent person.

honey wagon—a conveyance for carrying or spreading manure.

honey barge—garbage scow (navy).

honey bucket—a chamber pot.

honey man—a kept man.

honeycakes—a sweetheart.

hotcakes, sell like—*Hotcakes* (griddle cakes or pancakes) were at one time a very popular item at fairs, carnivals, and sporting events, selling in large quantities.

hot dogs—The people of Frankfurt, Germany, enjoyed a relatively thin sausage called "hot dachshund" because of its similarity in shape to the dachshund. This German breed of dog with its short legs and long body indeed looks quite a bit like a sausage. (*Dachshund* literally means badger dog.) The people of Vienna enjoyed these special sausages from Frankfurt, which they called *frankfurters.* Other Europeans called them *wieners,* the name that the Viennese call themselves.

In the United States, the *hot dog* was introduced at New York's Polo Grounds by concessionaire extraordinaire Harry M. Stevens in April 1900. It was first presented as a "hot dachshund" and served red-hot. The name was later shortened to *hot dachs* and finally Americanized to *hot dogs.*

The *hot dog* became so popular that its name is used today as an eatiom meaning very good, or superior. In the 1960s, *hot dog* developed still another meaning, that of a show-off.

huckleberry—The eatiom *huckleberry* has positive and negative definitions. A *huckleberry* can be a synonym for a man, fellow, or guy, probably what Mark Twain had in mind when he named Huckleberry Finn. *Huckleberry* has also, of late, come to mean a fool or jerk, but can also be a good-natured term of endearment. The *huckleberry,* also known as a whortleberry, is a shrub that produces sweet blue-black fruit.

humble pie—In the Middle Ages, *humble pie,* which was then called umble pie, was a very large pie filled with the less appetizing parts of a deer, such as the heart, brain, liver, and entrails. It was served to the servants in the kitchen while the noblemen and -women in the main hall were dining on venison.

The word *humble,* meaning lowly, was substituted for the medieval English word *umble,* meaning entrails, because of the similarity in their sound and sense. Eating *umble pie* was something that was forced upon the servants, who had to suffer this indignity because of their station in life. This was a humbling experience for the servants, just as today's metaphorical *humble pie* is humiliating.

hunger / hunger, from—There are numerous meanings for the expression *from hunger,* ranging from inferior, unpleasant, contemptible, unwanted, or ugly to cheap, lowbrow, disliked, corny, and hammy.

Hunger, which is truly *from hunger,* is derived from the Old English word *hungrig* and has no connection with the country named Hungary.

J

jam / jam-up / jam session—The word *jam* is derived from an Old English word that means to press or wedge things between two surfaces. Such is the case of the fruit being crushed into jam.

   jam—a sorry plight; a bad position to be in; a tightly packed group of people, cars, and so forth.

   jam-up—same as above.

   jam session—a group of musicians playing, usually without sheet music and for their own enjoyment.

jelly / jelly bean / jelly-belly / jelly roll—*Jelly* is derived from the Latin word *gelata,* a shortened version of *res gelata,* something frozen.

   Around 1905 the *jelly bean,* a small bean-shaped confection with a gelatinous center encased in a hard sugar coating, became popular.

Soon after its introduction, these colorful little candies produced their own eatioms based upon their similarity in shape to the human head (see *bean*), their color, and their gelatinous center.

jelly bean—a fancy dresser; an ignorant person; a novice baseball player.

jelly—*gravy* (which see); something achieved with little effort; a cinch.

jelly-belly—a fat person.

jelly roll—a womanizer.

juice / juiced / juice up / moo-juice / juice, stew in one's own—*Au jus,* a French term meaning with juice, refers to the culinary practice wherein a meat is served in its natural juice or gravy. In point of fact, the word *juice* can be traced to the Sanskrit word *yus,* meaning broth. *Yus* was the source of the Latin word *jus,* meaning juice.

juice—alcoholic beverage; electricity; currency, money; influence, power, leverage.

juiced—drunk.

juice up—energize, strengthen.

moo-juice—milk.

stew in one's own juice—to experience problems created by one's own doing. This expression originally referred to someone who was burned at the stake, a cruel medieval punishment. Chaucer used a similar expression, *to fry in one's own grease,* in his *Canterbury Tales* to describe the burning of a person at the stake.

junket / junk / junkie / junk food / junk bond / junk mail / junk call—The word *junk,* meaning useless or worthless stuff, is derived from the Old Portuguese word *junco,* a reed or rush, a fact that relates it to *junket,* a custard or cream cheese. *Junket* is a diminutive of *junk* and was so called because it was originally carried to market in reed (*juncata*) baskets.

junket—a short trip; a trip made by a politician on public funds, probably derived from the junket basket (or custard it contained) that might accompany someone taking a short trip. It is also possible that *junket*'s origin was the Portuguese word *junco,* which in turn came from the Malaysian word *jong,* a Chinese sailing boat originally made of reeds.

junk—drugs, especially heroin.

junkie—a drug addict.

junk food—food that is high in calories but low in nutrients.

junk bond—a corporate bond with a low rating.

junk mail—commercial mail that is unsolicited.

junk call—an unsolicited commercial telephone call.

kidney / kidney, of that / kidney-buster—The kidney's shape has caused it to be associated with similarly shaped items such as beans and pools.

of that kidney—of that temperament. This eatiom can be traced to the thirteenth century, and later appeared in the works of Shakespeare.

kidney-buster—a rough road; a hard-riding truck or bus.

kosher—The Yiddish word *kosher* is derived from the Hebrew word *kasher,* meaning fitting, proper, or ritually clean. In the Orthodox Jewish religion, *kosher* refers to the laws governing dietary fitness, but along with many other Yiddish words, it's been borrowed by the English language and has developed the idiomatic sense of something genuine or proper.

kraut / krauthead—*Kraut* or *krauthead,* ethnic slurs used to describe a German soldier, plane, or tank, are generally listed in dictionaries as *offensive.* The use of these derogatory terms is based upon the German fondness for sauerkraut (sour cabbage).

lard / larder / lard-bucket / lard, tub of / lard-ass / lardaceous—*Lard,* a pig's back fat, has become synonymous with any kind of fat.

   larder—a pantry; a room where lard and foods are stored.

   lard-bucket—a fat person.

   tub of lard—a fat person.

   lard-ass—a person having an unusually large rear end.

   lardaceous—lardy or fatlike.

lemon / lemon laws—In 1910 the Mills Novelty Company produced a slot machine with a gum vending attachment. Whether you won or lost, you received a piece of gum in one of the following flavors: lemon, spearmint, orange, and plum. Later, the bonus gum was dropped, but the gum symbols remain in use on many of today's Vegas-type slot machines.

The lemon, in combination with any other symbol, always signified that the player lost, and the word *lemon,* therefore, developed the sense of something bad, unpleasant, or faulty. The lemon's negative connotation was applied to defective automobiles, and in the 1980s the so-called *lemon law* was passed that required auto manufacturers to refund the cost of cars that proved to be poorly made.

lettuce / cabbage / kale / spinach / lettuce green—In 1861, Salmon P. Chase, Abraham Lincoln's Secretary of the Treasury, issued the first paper money printed by the U.S. government to finance the Union's effort during the Civil War. Chase, for reasons obscure to historians, printed the reverse side of these bills with green ink. These paper bills, which later lost their value, were called greenbacks by the northern troops who received them. The greening of paper money by Chase led to our currency's colorful nicknames, including *greenbacks, lettuce, kale, spinach,* and *cabbage.*

Lettuce green is a color similar in hue to the lettuce leaf.

licorice / licorice stick—A member of the pea family, *licorice* is a perennial herb grown in southern Europe along the Mediterranean coast and in the United States, used as a flavoring agent in medicines because of its masking qualities, as well as in candy.

The special licorice taste is imparted by a substance called glycyrrhizin, for which the Greek name is *glykyrrhiza*. *Licorice* is actually a corruption of this Greek word, which literally means sweet root. *Licorice stick* is a jazz term for a clarinet, presumably because of that instrument's similarity in appearance to the popular black-colored licorice most commonly produced.

lime / limey / lime-juicer—*Lime,* the name of a member of the citrus family, can be traced back to *limun,* an ancient Persian word for this fruit, as well as its close relative, *lemon* (which see). *Lime* or *lime green* is a shade of pale green that is so called because of the distinctive color of the *lime*. *Limelight,* a nineteenth-century theatrical spotlight, has nothing to do with the fruit.

In the eighteenth century, the British navy provided a daily ration of limes for Her Majesty's sailors while they were at sea, because doctors had discovered that the juice of the lime added ascorbic acid to the seamen's diet. This dietary supplement prevented scurvy, a disease that caused spongy and bleeding gums, eventually leading to the loss of teeth. As a result of this unusual addition to the English seamen's diet, British ships were known as *lime-juicers* and British sailors were referred to as *limeys*. In time, *limey* became widely used as a derogatory slang nickname for all British subjects.

lollipop (also **lollypop**)—The *lolli-* part of this word can be traced to an English dialect word for tongue, *lolly,* which is related to the word *loll,* to thrust one's tongue out in a pendulous manner. The *-pop* probably relates to the fact that you pop it into the mouth.

Lucullan—Before the fall of the Roman Empire, Lucius Licinius Lucullus was a general under Sulla, the dictator, and made so much money during his military career that he retired early. He then became so devoted to gracious living and throwing sumptuous parties that his name, in the form of *Lucullan,* became synonymous with *bacchanalian* (which see) feasts.

110

lunch / siesta / matinee / out to lunch / elevenses / lunch, eat someone's—*Lunch* was first derived from Scandinavian words that meant a lump, as in a lump of bread or such other food staple. The Spanish shaped this lump into their word *lonja,* a noon meal, although lunch was not always a noon meal as we know it today. *Noon,* in fact, is derived from the Latin *nona hora,* the ninth hour after daybreak, which is 3:00 P.M. *Siesta,* another Spanish word, is derived from *sexta hora,* the sixth hour after daybreak. *Matinee* is derived from the French word *matin,* meaning morning.

These various names for lunch and related periods of the day have done a bit of shifting as *lunch* became the noon meal, *siesta* became a brief nap after lunch, and *matinee* became an afternoon performance. *Out to lunch,* incidentally, is a slang phrase used to describe someone who is not mentally with it. The British have added one additional dining interlude, *elevenses,* a piece of cake with tea or coffee, taken at about eleven in the morning. And finally, *to eat someone's lunch* has come to mean to beat someone soundly.

macaroni/Macaroni—Unlike most pastas, macaroni is not named for its shape. *Macaroni,* instead, is derived from an Italian verb, *maccare,* which means to make a mixture or a jumble, such as a mixture of languages. Apparently, the food known as *macaroni* originally consisted of a mixture of things.

In the eighteenth century, a *Macaroni* was a member of the Macaroni Club in London, England. This club was composed of rich young dandies who put on continental airs and dressed flashily, primarily in the fashion of the Italians of that period. The Macaronis were noted for their insolence, as well as their love of drinking, gambling, and dueling. It was commonly believed that the Macaronis were named for their eclectic dress.

mackerel snapper (snatcher) / mackerel sky / mackerel, holy—In the days when Roman Catholics were prohibited from eating meat on Fridays, fish became a popular meat substitute. As a result, *mackerel snapper* became a popular slang term for Catholics in the U.S. No information could be found to explain why snapper or snatcher was preceded by mackerel and not some other fish. *Mackerel* is also used in the phrase *mackerel sky,* so called because of this sky's similarity to the mackerel's scales.

The mackerel, probably because of its association with the phrase *mackerel snapper,* is also used in the expression of surprise or wonder, *holy mackerel.*

manna—Theologians and historians have long been advancing theories on what the *manna* actually was that nourished the Israelites during their wanderings in the wilderness as told in the Book of Exodus. Apparently, even the children of Israel were not sure of what manna was since this word is derived from the Hebrew words *man hu,* which literally meant What is it? Manna may not have descended miraculously from heaven as is suggested in the biblical account, but rather from the dew or exudate of the tamarisk bush. *Manna* has come to mean anything badly needed that comes unexpectedly.

margarine—Margarine's inventor, Frenchman Hippolyte Megemouries, also coined the word for his butter substitute, *margarine,* which is a shortened form of the Greek phrase *margaron lithos,* meaning pearl stone or pearl. He explained that it was so named because of its pearly appearance.

marinara / marinade / marinate—The sea, or at least the ancient Latin word for it, *mare,* was the source of several eatioms that have seeped into modern English usage.

  marinara—This highly seasoned sauce of tomatoes, onions, spices, and garlic is derived from the Italian *alla marinara,* meaning in the sailor style. *Marinara* is derived from the Latin word *marinus,* meaning sea, which is the source for the English word *marine.* The *marinara* sauce was, apparently, a specialty of sailors plying the Mediterranean Sea.

  marinade—a brine made of wine or vinegar, oil, various herbs, and spices in which fish, fowl, and meat may be soaked before cooking.

Marinade is related to *marinara* and is likewise derived from the word *mare*. The pickling (see *pickle*) process probably served to preserve the meat, or at least disguise spoilage, so that the food would be palatable on long sea voyages.

marinate—to steep in a marinade.

matters of taste—This treatise is devoted to words that we use to describe those who have taste and those who abuse it.

connoisseur—a person with discriminating taste concerning the arts and food. The term is derived from the Old French word *connoistre,* by way of the Latin word *cognoscere,* to know.

epicure—a person with refined taste, especially in food and wine. *Epicure* is derived from *Epicurus,* an ancient Greek (300 B.C.) who held that refined sensuousness was beneficial.

gastronome—a connoisseur of good food and drink—from the French word *gastronomie,* which is derived from the Greek word *gaster,* belly.

115

glutton—a person who has a great appetite for food or just about anything else. It is derived from the Latin words *gluttire,* to swallow, and *gluttus,* the throat.

gourmet—a connoisseur of fine food and drink. *Gourmet* is derived from the medieval French word *gromet,* a servant, a wine merchant, or his assistant. *Gromet* went on to become *groom,* a young servant. *Gourmand,* a derivative of *gourmet,* is one who loves food and drink and partakes of it heartily and often to excess.

hedonist—one who holds that pleasure is the chief good. *Hedonist* is derived from the Greek word *hedone,* meaning pleasure.

Sybarite—a person devoted to pleasure and luxury. This word was derived from *Sybaris,* the name of an ancient Greek colony located in Italy (700 B.C.) and notorious for the luxury enjoyed by its inhabitants.

mealymouthed/meal ticket—A person who is not straightforward in speech, avoids the use of plain language, and is evasive or hypocritical is said to be *mealymouthed.* This eatiom, according to the late John Ciardi's book, *A Browser's Dictionary,* is derived from the Old German expression *Mehl im Maule behalten,* which literally describes persons who are unable or unwilling to speak for fear that the meal they are eating might fall out of their mouths.

Meal also describes coarse unsifted grain powder. A mouthful of meal or anything that is mealy would, indeed, make talking difficult. *Meal* in this case is derived from the Latin word *molere,* meaning to grind.

The *meal* in *meal ticket* comes from a different source, the Gothic or Old Nordic word *mel,* meaning time of day. A *meal ticket* was simply a ticket that entitled its owner to meals in a specified restaurant at reduced prices. Members of circus troops were also issued tickets that entitled them to free meals in the circus's dining tent. Today, however, a *meal ticket* is someone or something upon which a person is dependent for his or her livelihood.

meat / meat, cold / meat, dead / meatball / meat wagon / meathead / meat, raw / meat hooks /

meat-ax / meaty—*Meat,* a word derived directly from the Old English word *mete,* can be traced all the way back to its Indo-European root word *mad,* meaning to be moist. It is probably also related to the Greek word for breast, *mastos. Meat's* earlier use was as a generic term for food.

cold meat—a dead person.

dead meat—someone who because of an unfortunate act of omission or commission will be rendered totally useless; washed up; ruined; destroyed.

meatball—a clumsy or ineffectual person.

meat wagon—ambulance.

meathead—a stupid person.

raw meat—one who is easily defeated or defrauded. This term stems from the way in which a hungry carnivore eagerly consumes a piece of raw meat.

meat hooks—the hands or fists.

meat-ax—drastic or severe approach.

meaty—rich in content.

mellow / mellow out / mellow yellow / mollify / mellifluous—*Mellow* is derived from the Latin word *molere,* to grind into flour, and the Old English word *melu,* meaning meal or flour.

mellow—soft, ripe, mature; pleasantly drunk; calm, peaceful; a state induced by drugs.

mellow out—to become completely relaxed.

mellow yellow—a species of LSD; a young mulatto female (offensive).

mollify—to calm; placate. *Mollify* is derived from *mollificare,* which literally means to soften meal.

Mellifluous is another ancient eatiom that was elevated over the years to the status of standard English. *Mellifluous* is not, however, derived from *meal* but combines instead *mel,* meaning honey, and *fluere,* to flow. *Mellifluous* describes, among other things, the sweetly flowing language of a good writer or orator.

melon (pie), cut (slice) the / melon (pumpkin) head—Slicing up a pie or melon is used metaphorically for dividing profits, bonuses, and dividends. The pie is also used as a graph in which the size of each slice represents a percentage of the whole pie (100 percent).

To the ancient Greeks, a watermelon was a *melopepon,* a word that combines *melon,* meaning apple, and *pepon,* meaning large. The *pepon* eventually grew into the English word *pumpkin* (which see). The pumpkin's human-head shape resulted in the *melon (pumpkin) head* eatiom, which describes a slow-witted person.

meshuga—The ancient Hebrew word from which *cider* is derived, *shekar,* was originally defined as a strong alcoholic beverage, and is related to another Hebrew word, *shagah,* to be intoxicated. A new twist was given to *shagah* when it was adopted by the Yiddish language as *meshuga,* someone who is insane or crazy, a condition often brought about by strong drink.

mess / mess around / mess up / mess hall—The medieval English word *mes,* a meal or course thereof, is the source of its modern counterpart, *mess. Mes,* in turn, can be traced to the Latin word *missus,* meaning "what is sent out." The dirty or untidy sense of *mess* is undoubtedly derived from the condition of a dining table or room after a meal has been consumed.

mess—a large amount of anything.

mess around—to act without purpose; to fool around.

mess up—to work poorly; to screw up.

mess hall—an eating place.

milksop / sop / milky / milk / milk run / milk of human kindness—The word *sop* is derived from the Anglo-Saxon word *sopp,* meaning bread dunked into a liquid. *Sop* is related to sup, supper, and soup. Later, a *sop* was something given to a child as a pacifier, and currently *sop* is used as a noun to describe a person who is spineless or lacking in willpower. The ultimate *sop,* in this sense, is the *milksop,* essentially a military term that describes a person who sops milk and is therefore infantile and unfit for combat.

Milk is derived from the Latin word *mulgere,* meaning to drain.

milky—something that has a milky consistency or that is white in color.

milk—to get the very most one can out of a situation; to exploit something to the fullest.

milk run—a plane or train or other vehicle that has many stops such as one that picks up or delivers milk in bulk at every station along its way.

milk of human kindness—compassion, understanding, based upon a mother's nourishment of her baby with the milk from her own breast.

mincemeat / mincemeat, make / mince words, not to / mincing steps or manners / mince pie / mince matters, not to—*Mincemeat* is, apparently, another example of a concoction by which medieval cooks thought to make animal innards more palatable (see *humble pie*). *Mincemeat* was originally a mixture of minced suet and innards such as ox heart, flavored with chopped apples, currants, candied citron, and a sprinkling of raisins.

make mincemeat—to destroy completely.

not to mince words—to speak frankly or honestly.

mincing steps or manners—very delicate.

mince pie—usually served at Christmastime.

not to mince matters—to speak forthrightly.

mishmash—*Mishmash* is a reduplication, a word that often combines rhyme and alliteration. The origin of its second element, *-mash* (the source of *mish-* is unknown and is likely a close duplication of *-mash*), is the Anglo-Saxon word *masc,* a mixture of ground grains and other foods. Today, a *mishmash* is a messy confusion of things, a *hodgepodge* (which see), or a jumble.

molasses—The high viscosity of molasses is responsible for its use as a simile for things that are as slow or thick as this honeylike substance produced during the refining of sugar or from sorghum. Molasses, which varies in color from a light to dark brown, ultimately derives its name from the Latin word *mel,* meaning honey, and is used as an eatiom for a good-looking used automobile prominently displayed to attract customers to a used-car lot. Sorghum itself is a syrup made from the sweet juice of the stems of *sorgo,* a cereal grass used to make sugar and as a fodder.

Viscose and *viscosity* were originally derived

123

from the Latin word *viscum,* a birdlime made from mistletoe berries. Birdlime was applied to the twigs and branches of trees and bushes to entrap birds in the sticky stuff. They were then removed and used as food. The use of birdlime to catch birds for human consumption has been long since banned by most countries.

morsel/remorse—Here is a juicy *tidbit* (which see), the *morsel,* which is defined as a small piece of food or candy, but which has developed the sense of a small quantity of just about anything. *Morsel* is a diminutive form derived from the Latin word *mordere,* to bite. This early eatiom is closely related to another antiquated eatiom, *remorse,* which literally means to bite back (the way one's conscience does after one commits a wrong).

mousse/mousseline—*Mousse* is a sweet success story that has recently turned into a hair-raising one as well. A *mousse* is a frothy dessert made with whipped cream, egg whites, flavoring, and occasionally gelatin, and frequently mixed with fruits. *Mousse* is derived from the Latin word *mulsa,* fermented honey or wine, and is related to the Latin word *mel,* meaning honey. More recently, of course, a line of foamy hair products designed to keep hairdos in place has reached the market. These new hair-care preparations are classified as *mousses. Mousseline* has nothing to do with hair products, but is a French version of a cotton fabric, also called muslin, based on its place of origin, Musol, Iraq.

moxie—While the word *moxie* is often assumed to be of Yiddish origin, it was actually derived from the name of a soft drink first bottled in New England in 1884.

Moxie, which is listed in the dictionary as a lowercase noun as well as a trademark, is still in production. It has been described as a bitter carbonated herbal drink or a tart cola similar to root beer.

This American slang original, *moxie,* has come to mean courage of a high order. How did the name for this soft drink produce its gutsy slang offspring? The most convincing theory is that because of its bitterness it took a great deal of courage to drink it. The word *moxie* was probably derived from a New England place name.

mush / mush-head / mush mouth / mushy / masher
—*Mush,* a variant of *mash* from the Old English word *masc,* meaning to mash, describes the consistency of the thing mashed. *Mush* eatomizes into these definitions: incessant or excessive talk; bunk; nonsense; the mouth; the face; anything that is excessively sentimental.

mush-head—a silly or foolish person.

mush mouth—one who talks as if he has mush in his mouth—indistinctly.

mushy—corny; overly sentimental.

masher—one who makes unwanted advances toward women in public places, and uses a very *mushy* line to achieve his amorous objective.

mushroom / mushroom cloud / mushroom slab construction—The mushrooms from which the following eatioms have *mushroomed* are the edible species of fungi, especially those of the *Agaricaceae* family.

mushroom—to spread rapidly, like the fungi.

mushroom cloud—a smoke cloud or a radioactive cloud produced by an atomic explosion, so called because of its resemblance to a mushroom.

mushroom slab construction—a beamless reinforced-concrete floor-and-roof construction employing columns with widely flaring heads or capitals.

mustard, (not) cut the—In the early part of the nineteenth century, to be the *proper mustard* was a popular phrase apparently based upon the great disparity in the quality of mustards available at the time. This eatiom, which essentially means to do (or not do) something well, is derived from the notion of being able to actually cut the mustard plant, or being able to achieve "the proper mustard."

mutton / lamb / sheep / muttonhead / mutton-top—*Sheep* is the name of a wool-bearing ungulate while it is still on the hoof. As soon as the sheep is slaughtered and dressed to be cooked and served as food it is called *mutton. Lamb,* on the other hand, is a young sheep (up to a year of age), as well as the word for the food that it provides.

Sheep and *lamb* were introduced to England,

linguistically speaking, by the Anglo-Saxons, but *mutton* is of French origin via the Celts (Gauls). Etymologists attribute the linguistic survival of *sheep* and *lamb* to the fact that the Anglo-Saxons continued to raise and cook the meat of these animals for their French rulers long after the Norman invasion of England in 1066.

It is interesting to note that the English use the word *lamb* to describe an innocent, gentle, or weak person. *Sheep,* too, is used idiomatically to describe a defenseless, innocent, docile, or stupid person. *Mutton* survives in the derogatory *mutton-head* or *mutton-top* eatioms, which also describe a stupid person.

noodle(s) / noodle-work / noodle-head / noodle-twister / limp noodle—*Noodles,* derived from the German word *nudel* (of obscure origin), are narrow strips of unleavened dough rolled thin and dried. They are then boiled and served alone or in soups and casseroles. Despite the fact that this ribbon-shaped pasta bears no resemblance to the head, the *noodle* has become a slang synonym for the human head (*using your noodle*). In this context *noodle* also means to play or toy with, to improvise or to tamper with. But while *noodle-work* is defined as thinking or studying, a *noodle-head* is a foolish or stupid person. A *noodle-twister,* however, is cigar-industry jargon for someone who rolls cigars by hand. A *limp noodle* is something or someone that is ineffectual, weak, or tasteless.

nosh/snack—*Nosh* is a Yiddish tidbit derived from *nashn,* meaning to gnaw, nibble. To *nosh* is to eat *snacks* between meals. *Snack* is a derivative of the Middle English word *snachen,* meaning to snatch or snap like a dog's bite, but it later developed the sense of a quick bite of food, usually taken between meals.

nut / nut house / nut hatch / nut farm / nut college / nuts about / nutty / nutso / nutty as a fruitcake / nuts, soup to / nuts / nerts (nertz) / filbert / nut to crack, tough (hard)—At the core of this long list of nutty eatioms is the Latin word *nux,* a nut. Its derivative, *nucleus,* meaning a kernel, is responsible for the French word *nucléaire,* which was anglicized to *nuclear.*

> **nut**—the human head; an insane person; an eccentric person; a fanatic; expense or overhead; a term of affection.

> **nut house**—an institution for the insane.

> **nut hatch**—same meaning as *nut house.*

> **nut farm**—same meaning as *nut house.*

> **nut college**—same meaning as *nut house.*

> **nuts about**—to be very enthusiastic about; to be in love.

nutty—eccentric.

nutso—same meaning as *nutty*.

nutty as a fruitcake—eccentric.

soup to nuts—a full-course meal; everything from A to Z.

nuts—to reject completely.

nerts (nertz)—a variant of *nuts*.

filbert—a thick-shelled edible variety of the hazelnut, occasionally used as a jocular synonym for an eccentric. The *filbert* is so named because the nuts are said to ripen on Saint Philbert's Day (August 22).

tough (hard) nut to crack—a difficult problem to solve; a tough-minded person who is unwilling to confess to something or be dissuaded; one who is difficult to defeat.

oats, sow wild / oats, feel one's—One rarely hears the expression *to sow wild oats* used in connection with a woman. The metaphor, which means to carry on in a wild, youthful, and uninhibited way, can be traced to the British Isles, where wild oats are a weed; and to spend precious time sowing such a worthless crop would be a frivolous waste of a man's youth (as well as a woman's). *To feel one's oats* is an animal metaphor that means to be lively or frisky and is derived from the fact that horses become very spirited after eating oats.

onion / onions, know one's / onion dome / onion-skin / onion, off one's—The word *onion* is derived from the Latin word *unus,* meaning one. The onion's original "oneness" sense is due to the fact that it is composed of many individual layers that make up one unit. A member of the amaryllis family, the onion has a strong taste and odor, which is attributed to a stimulating oil. Mongolia

was the birthplace of the onion; it wasn't cultivated in the U.S. until 1750. The most popular
onions are the Danvers, Southport, Bermuda, red
globe, brown, Spanish, and Vidalia. The Vidalia is
a mild variety grown in Vidalia, Georgia, where
the soil imparts a special sweetness to this onion.

know one's onions—to be knowledgeable
about a specific subject or special field of en-
deavor.

onion dome—an onion-shaped domed roof
used as an architectural feature on Russian Orthodox churches. The beautiful Saint Basil's
church in Moscow possesses the best example
of these domes.

onionskin—a thin lightweight translucent paper used for making carbon copies. Since the
advent of photocopying machines, the use of
onionskin paper has steadily declined.

off one's onion—the onion is synonymous
with *head,* and to be off one's onion is to be
crazy.

Oreo (oreo) cookie—In the late 1960s, Whitney
Young, Jr., an executive of the Urban League,

was called an *oreo* by an anonymous militant black who was unhappy with the slow progress of black civil rights organizations in gaining better conditions for their people. Oreo, best known as the trademark for a cream-filled chocolate cookie, came in use as a derogatory term for a black person denying his or her heritage to take on characteristically middle-class white attitudes, values, and behavior.

oyster, the world is my / oyster part—Oysters yield pearls and, therefore, the oyster shell represents a little world of potential value. So, when people say, *"The world is my oyster,"* it means that things are going well for them because they perceive their world as being full of promise and potential.

As to the rule that oysters should be eaten only in a month having an *r* in its spelling, oysters are seldom harvested in May, June, July, or August (months without an *r*) because it is during these months that oysters spawn. Therefore, oysters are generally not available to the public at that time of the year.

It is also important to note that the English word *ostracize,* meaning to banish someone from a particular society, is derived from the same root word as *oyster*.

In theatrical slang, an *oyster part* is one in which the actor has only one line to speak.

pan / pancake turner / panhandler / pancake land-ing / pan out / pan, on the—Whether you call them hotcakes, griddle cakes, flapjacks, slapjacks, flannel cakes, battercakes, johnnycakes, corncakes, hoecakes, or *pancakes,* depends, to a great extent, upon what part of the country you hail from. The word *pancake,* however, is derived from a very old cooking pan or bowl that the Romans called a *patina,* which they used to make flat cakes.

> **pan**—the human face; a bad criticism or review. This latter sense is probably derived from the phrase *pan out* (below).

> **pancake turner**—a disc jockey.

> **panhandler**—a person who wields or handles a pan, cup, hat, or other receptacle in which to collect alms.

pancake landing—an airplane landing that results in an abrupt plop as opposed to a graceful glide.

pan out—a good or bad result, derived from the use of a pan to mine grains of gold in a stream. If the pan yielded sand, but no gold, it was said that it did not *pan out* well.

on the pan—someone or something that receives negative criticism.

pap—*Pap,* a word defined as soft food suitable for infants, is also used eatiomatically to describe talk, ideas, books, and the like that are infantile or that have little substance and are therefore of little value to adults.

Pap has two possible sources. The first is the Latin word *pappa,* a child's word for food, and the second, the Latin word *papilla,* meaning nipple. Both words are probably echoic (words that mimic sound) and are traceable to the earliest Indo-European root words.

Closely related to the *pap* words above is *pabulum,* a word derived intact from Latin, which means food or nourishment. At one time a condensed form of the word, *Pablum,* was used as a trademark for a baby cereal.

pasta—That the words *pasta* and *paste* are related etymologically will not come as a surprise to most people. Both words were derived from the Latin word *pasta,* meaning a paste or dough made with flour that was eventually used to make spaghetti, macaroni, and other pastas. According to sources, a spaghettilike pasta was first prepared by the Chinese circa 1000 B.C. Legend attributes the introduction of spaghetti into Europe to Marco Polo and his uncle and father toward the end of the thirteenth century. The Italians produced a wide range of pasta types, which were generally named after their shapes.

spaghetti—little cords; strings.

lasagna—a large flat rectangle strip of pasta derived from the Latin word meaning baking pot. They are baked in layers, usually with ground meat and cheese.

vermicelli—little worms.

ravioli—little turnips.

cannelloni—little tubes—usually filled with poultry, meat, or cheese and baked in a cream sauce.

mostaccioli—little mustaches.

linguine—little tongues.

peach / peachy / peachy-keen / peacherino / peach fuzz / peaches and cream—The universal acceptance of, and pleasure derived from, the fruit of the *Prunus persica* tree is evidenced by the numerous *peachy* eatioms that have fallen from it. I am talking, of course, about the *peach*. That the word *peach* emanated from Persia is incontrovertible. In fact, the name for this fruit is an elliptical (shortened) version of the Greek words *Persikon melon* (see *melon*), which means apple of Persia. *Persikon* was reshaped through the ages as it was translated through Latin (*persicum*), Old French (*pesche*), and medieval English (*peche*), which brought us to the English (*peach*).

peach—a person or thing that is especially nice, enjoyable, or attractive.

peachy—a word having the same positive sense as *peach* above.

peachy-keen—same meaning as *peach* and *peachy* above.

peacherino—The *-erino* ending can be traced to the Spanish and Italian *-ino* word endings. Same sense as the three previous eatioms.

peach fuzz—the first fuzzy growth of facial hair on a boy or young man, because of its resemblance to the fuzz on a peach.

peaches and cream—something pleasant—often used to describe a lovely complexion.

peanuts / peanut gallery / goober / goober grabber/ goober grease—In the antebellum South the *peanut* was known as a *goober,* which is the Congolese word for this vegetable that masquerades as a nut. The plantation slaves were simply using their native word, *goober,* for the peanut. This explains why the use of the goober sobriquet is still generally confined to the South. The first element in *peanut, pea-,* should prepare you for the revelation that the *peanut* is not a true nut at all, but a member of the pea family. Like other peas, the seeds grow in a pod, but unlike the regular pea they develop underground.

peanuts—a small sum of money.

peanut gallery—the top balcony of a theater where its occupants presumably dine on peanuts.

goober-grabber—a Georgia native.

goober grease—peanut butter.

pea soup / pea / pea jacket—The *pea* provides us with a delicious thick fiber-rich soup usually made from dried split peas. Its traditional thickness resulted in its use as an eatiom for a very thick yellowish fog associated with London, England. The *pea* is also eatiomatic for a baseball, golf ball, and a bullet. The *pea jacket,* a hip-length, double-breasted coat made of heavy wool and traditionally worn by seamen, is an example of folk (false) etymology and is derived from the Dutch word *pijjekker,* or coarse jacket. The *pij-* became anglicized to *pea.*

pepper / pepper and salt / pepper pot / pepper game / pep / pep talk / pep rally / peppy / pep up—Pepper's ability to perk up the taste of food has given rise to a variety of *peppy* eatioms, all of which were derived from the Greek word *peperi.*

pepper—a personality trait exemplified by *pep* or vitality; to throw a baseball with great velocity.

pepper and salt—something, such as a head of hair, that is speckled with contrasting colors (black and white).

pepper pot—a box with holes in its top through which ground pepper is sprinkled; a person with a tempestuous personality; a type of soup.

pepper game—a warm-up procedure used in baseball in which a batter bunts baseballs to fielders standing nearby.

pep—vitality.

pep talk—a speech or talk designed to arouse enthusiasm.

pep rally—a gathering, usually before an athletic event, designed to arouse team spirit among supporters and athletes alike.

peppy—the condition of being upbeat or enthusiastic.

pep up—to stimulate or excite.

percolator/percolate—In the 1920s, an electric appliance called the Per-O-Toaster, manufactured by the Armstrong Company, was the first to automatically brew coffee by infusion or percolation.

Percolate is derived from the Latin word *percolare* (*per-*, through, and *-colare,* to strain or filter through) and has these additional meanings: to become heated; to boil over, as with an automobile engine; to operate efficiently or smoothly; to think intelligently or efficiently; to stroll, walk, or saunter.

pickle—Some etymologists believe that the *pickle* is an eponym (a word derived from a person's name) based upon the name of a fourteenth-century Dutch fisherman or fishmonger by the name of William Buekel. Buekel, it is said, first preserved fish in vinegar brine. Much later, in the eighteenth century, cucumbers and other vegetables were preserved and flavored in the same way. The alternate derivation of the *pickle* is the fourteenth-century Dutch word *pekel,* meaning pickle or brine. Perhaps the *pekel* was derived from, or reinforced by, William's purported involvement with food preservation. *Pickle,* an awkward or dif-

143

ficult situation, is also used to describe a sour, unpleasant, or unfriendly person.

picnic—*Picnic,* which has come to mean something very easy (see *cake, piece of; pie, easy as*), combines the French word *piquer,* to pick at something (often with a sharp instrument), and *nique,* a worthless thing.

pie / magpie / pie, easy as / pie, nice as / pie, cutie / pie sweetie / apple pie / pie-eyed / pie, piece of the / pie in the sky / pie chart / pieface—The word *pie* is derived from the Latin word *pica,* for *magpie,* a bird akin to the woodpecker. The magpie has two distinctive traits. First, it is a noisy chatterer, and second, it is known to be a collector of diverse bits and pieces.

In medieval England, *magpie* was shortened to *pie,* which came to be defined also as a food dish prepared with meat or fish and covered with pastry. The popular assumption among etymologists is that the magpie was an early and popular filling for this medieval pastry dish, and a piece of its name became associated with pies in general.

easy as pie—Because of the pleasant experience of eating a piece of pie, and the ease with which we do so, this eatiom has come to mean something that is extremely easy to do.

nice as pie—a simile that compares the pleasant nature of eating a pie to someone who is extremely well behaved.

cutie pie—a term of endearment usually reserved for a small child or a pretty young woman.

sweetie pie—same as *cutie pie.*

apple pie—a reference to old-fashioned American values.

pie-eyed—a slang term for someone who is drunk, because of the often wide-eyed look of those in an intoxicated state.

piece of the pie—a share in a financial venture (see *pie chart*, below).

pie in the sky—a future reward that people hope to receive in heaven though it has eluded them on earth. *Pie* is a symbol for good living while *sky* represents heaven. Today, *pie in the* *sky* means an illusory promise of future benefits.

pie chart—a chart (graph) in the shape of a circle divided into pie-shaped segments with the relative shares or quantities represented by proportionately different-sized slices.

pieface—an ignorant or foolish person.

pineapple / pineapple, Chicago—The pineapple, the edible fruit of a tropical plant, is thought to have originated in Brazil. The fruit was so named because of its similarity in appearance to the pinecone, which had been called a *pineapple* long before the discovery of its juicier namesake.

In World War I, *pineapple* was adopted as a slang name for the hand grenade because of their similar appearance. And later, during the Prohibition Era (1920–1933), hand grenades were called *Chicago pineapples* because of their use by, and association with, that city's gangsters.

plate full, have one's / plateful / plate, off one's / plat du jour—*Plate* is derived from the Greek word *plateia,* something flat. Words such as *plateau* and *platypus,* the flat-footed (*pous*) aquatic animal of

Australia and Tasmania, are derived from this Greek source.

have one's plate full—to be busy or fully occupied. The reference here is to a full plate of food.

plateful—a large quantity.

off one's plate—no longer one's concern or responsibility.

plat du jour—dish of the day (French).

plum—The word *plum* is derived from the late Latin word *prunus,* the prune tree (a member of the rose family), and it is from the special variety of *plum* that dries without spoiling that we get the prune. The plum, which was probably first discovered in Asia Minor, has the eatiomatic sense of a good thing.

The reward connotation of *plum* is traceable to a venerable English legend that is captured in a Mother Goose rhyme about Thomas (Jack) Horner. Horner, as this story goes, was the steward for the bishop of Glastonbury Cathedral, who sent Jack to London with twelve deeds to valuable properties that he was to present to King Henry VIII. These deeds, a gift from the bishop to his monarch, were placed in a large Christmas pie for safekeeping. On his way to London, according to legend, Horner, lifting the pie crust, also "lifted" one of the deeds, a real *plum,* which he kept for himself.

pork / pork barrel / pork chopper / pork chop / porker / porky—Since the late nineteenth century, the word *pork* has been used in slang parlance for graft, because of pork's high content of fat and grease, words associated with graft. Fat is also used in a political sense in the *slush fund* (which see), a phrase that is also derived from animal fat. *Pork barrel* politics are still very popular with members of the U.S. Congress. *Pork barrel* legislation is a congressional bill designed to provide funding for local (district or state) improvements at federal government expense. Such legislation is designed to ingratiate a lawmaker with his constituents.

pork chopper—a labor official who is placed on a union payroll because of past services rendered to that union, but who is required to do little work; a union official motivated by self-interest.

pork chop—the fringe benefits that union members hope to get as a result of a strike.

porker—a fat person.

porky—saucy, cocky, presumptuous; also a fat person.

porridge / porridge bowl / porridge disturber / porridge, sip one's last—*Porridge,* which is described as an oatmeal of grain or cereal boiled in water or milk to a thick gruel, is similar to, and a corruption of, *pottage,* something made in a pot.

porridge—to cook porridge; to conjure up and execute a plan.

porridge bowl—the stomach.

porridge disturber—a blow to the stomach.

sip one's last porridge—to die.

pot, gone to / potboiler / potbelly / potshot / potlicker / pot liquor / pothouse / pot-valor / potwalloper / pot wrestler / pot massager / pot slinger / pot, sweeten

the / potluck / pot, melting / pot / pothead—For the most part, this mess of *pot* words is derived from the Latin word *potarium,* a drinking vessel, and is related to another Latin word *potare,* to drink.

gone to pot—something that is ruined, decayed, or devastated. There are at least four explanations for this eatiom: a pot in which scrap metal is melted; leftover meats and vegetables that have been diced up into a *hash* (which see); human ashes placed into an urn; a man or woman with a large *potbelly* (see below).

potboiler—a second-rate work of literature or art produced for immediate financial gain.

potbelly—a stomach shaped like a pot.

potshot—Years ago, when a family's next meal depended upon one's skill or luck as a hunter, a potshot was literally a shot fired at an animal, which was then taken home (if the shot was good), placed in the pot, and served for supper (dinner). Such a shot was generally fired at point-blank range, sometimes illegally, and always in a random or incidental manner. The random or incidental sense of such a shot was transferred to the idea of criticism directed at a nearby target without much thought and in a casual or haphazard manner.

potlicker—a disgusting or low person; one who originally survived by licking pots and from eating garbage pickings.

pot liquor—gravy; broth in which meat or vegetables have been cooked.

pothouse—a tavern where ale and other *pot*ent drinks are served.

pot-valor—courage derived from alcoholic beverages.

potwalloper—a cook (one who boils pots); a dishwasher.

pot wrestler—a cook or dishwasher.

pot massager—one who washes pots and pans.

pot slinger—a cook.

sweeten the pot—to put more money into a poker pot (analogous to sweetening a pot of food with additional ingredients).

potluck—food that happens to be on hand when guests arrive unexpectedly.

melting pot—a phrase whose eatiomatic sense is attributed to Israel Zangwill to describe the process whereby the U.S. welcomes people from the world over and gradually breaks down their ethnic barriers by creating a homogeneous mixture through intermarriage.

pot—marijuana. *Pot* is a shortened variation of the Mexican-Spanish phrase, *potacion de quay* (drink of grief), in which marijuana buds have been soaked in wine.

pothead—a marijuana addict.

potato, hot / potatoes, meat and / potatoes, small / hot patootie / potato / potato head—The sweet potato was first discovered in the Caribbean by the Spaniards, who used the native word for it, *batata.* When the white potato was later found in Peru, it, too, was called a *batata,* albeit erroneously. The word *batata* was eventually anglicized to *potato.*

hot potato—a difficult matter to handle; something risky or unpleasant.

small potatoes—something of little importance. *No small potatoes,* on the other hand, describes a thing that is no easy matter.

meat and potatoes—Since shortly after World War II this expression has come to mean something that is fundamental; basic. This sense is, undoubtedly, due to the fact that meat and potatoes are essential components in the majority of meals. A *meat-and-potatoes* man (or woman) is very much down to earth.

hot patootie—a sexy woman. *Patootie* is a corruption of *potato,* possibly a combination of *potato* and *tootsie.*

potato—the head; the face; a dollar; a ball.

potato head—an ignorant person.

potpourri—*Potpourri* has a variety of meanings, including a mixture of fragrant flowers or flower petals and spices; a musical medley; a collection of literary selections; any mixture of objects that are unrelated. *Potpourri* is one word that has definitely improved with age since its beginning as the Spanish compound *olla podrida,* meaning rotten pot. The *olla podrida* origin suggests that at one time, before refrigeration, spoiled meat was disguised with spices to make it more palatable. *Podrida* is related to putrid. The French translation resulted in a conversion of the Spanish *olla* to *pot-* and *podrida* to -*pourri*—a combination that was finally borrowed unchanged by the English language.

precocious / apricot / half-baked—*Precocious* is an ancient eatiom derived from the Latin word *praecoquere,* meaning to precook. Along the way it developed its current sense of a child who is unusually advanced or mature for its age.

The *apricot,* surprisingly, developed from the same word tree as *precocious.* The word for this tart fruit came into English directly from the Arab word *burquoq,* which in turn was derived from *praecox,* a variant of *praecoquere,* which means early ripening. The Arabs added *al,* meaning the, and thus *al burquoq* became *apricot,* which ripens earlier than its close relative, the peach.

Half-baked is an antonym of *precocious* and describes someone or something that was not properly cooked and is therefore incomplete, lacking in experience, unrealistic, stupid, or half-witted.

pretzel/pretzel-bender—Two sources have been offered for the word *pretzel:* the Latin word *pretiole,* meaning little gift, and the Italian word *bracciatelli,* meaning small arms. The pretzel's origin is traced back to the Middle Ages, when, it is said, Italian monks gave them to children as a reward for learning their prayers. This popular *pretzel* origin supports the *pretiole* theory, while the traditional cross-armed shape of the *pretzel* sustains the *bracciatelli* hypothesis.

Pretzel is a pet name for a French horn, while a *pretzel-bender* refers to a peculiar or eccentric person, a French horn player, or a wrestler.

prune / prune face / prunes, full of / prune picker—The prune is a variety of *plum* (which see) that dries without spoiling.

prune—someone who is mentally retarded, prudish, scholarly, or eccentric.

prune face—Like the Dick Tracy villain, Pruneface, the eatiom describes a sad-looking or homely person.

full of prunes—a spirited person (see *beans, full of*)—a derogatory term suggesting that a person's logic is poor or reactions slow.

prune picker—a Californian, so called because of the many prune plum trees grown there.

pudding / pudding, proof of the / puddinghead— Hasty pudding was originally a British pudding or porridge consisting of oatmeal or flour boiled in water. (The New England recipe for hasty pudding consists of cornmeal mush usually served hot with milk and maple sugar or molasses.)

Although *pudding* was an English surname in the twelfth century, our word *pudding* is most likely derived from a thirteenth-century English word that described an animal's stomach or intestine used as a casing and filled with meat. Since the seventeenth century, pudding has in most cases lost its casing and come to mean a boiled or baked, sweetened or unsweetened dessert or food.

The only way to truly test how good (or bad) these puddings are would be to taste them. This sentiment was captured in the fifteenth-century proverb *The proof of the pudding is in the eating,* which wisely suggests that though something might appear to be tasty or look attractive, you will never truly be certain until you try it. A *puddinghead,* immortalized in Mark Twain's novel of

diner—the first *diners* were old or surplus dining cars sold off by the railroad companies.

rhubarb—Rhubarb is classified as a vegetable, but it is thought of as a fruit because it is often sweetened, stewed, and served as a pie filling or as a fruitlike dessert. The word *rhubarb* is also used as a slang term meaning to quarrel or squabble. Its special eatiomatic usage can be traced back to fourteenth-century England, when the word *rhubarb* was repeated by theater extras to re-create angry crowd noise.

Etymologists are involved in a *rhubarb* over the origin of *rhubarb*. Some experts suggest that the *rhu-* in this word stems from an ancient word meaning *root.* The majority, however, attribute the first element to *Rha,* an ancient name for the Volga River, which is derived from the Greek word *rhein,* meaning to flow. The *-barb* is derived from the Latin word *barbarum,* meaning barbarian. The combined sense is the plant from the barbarian region of the Volga River.

rice Christian—During the early stages of the Christian missions to China and India, hungry peasants embraced Christianity simply to obtain food (rice). Such converts were pejoratively called *rice Christians.* A parallel could be drawn between the *rice Christians* and those young men and women who attended church socials, not for purposes of the soul, but for the sole purpose of meeting suitable marriage partners.

Another example of the *rice Christian* is the *souper,* a homeless person who goes to a big city Christian mission for food, usually soup.

salad days—*Salad days* has a range of meanings that covers all of the bases. On the one hand it can mean one's best period of vigor, enthusiasm, and creativity; on the other it can mean a period of youthful inexperience or naïveté.

Salad days remains fresh after many years of use. In fact, Shakespeare used the naive sense of this expression in *Antony and Cleopatra* when he put these words into Cleo's mouth: ". . . my salad days, when I was green in judgment."

salmagundi—*Salary, salad, salami,* and *salmagundi* all have a common syllable, *sal-,* which, surprisingly, is derived from the Latin word for salt, *sal.* A *salmagundi* is a mixed dish consisting of chopped or cubed poultry, meat, or fish, together with eggs, anchovies, and onions, and served with vinegar and oil. It is a stewlike mixture that derives its name from a tasty mixing of the Italian word *salami,* meaning salt meat, and the Latin word *condire,* meaning to pickle. *Salmagundi* has developed the general sense of a mixture of any kind, a miscellany, and is eatiomatically synonymous with *potpourri, hodgepodge,* and *mishmash* (all of which see).

salt, (not) worth one's / salt, take with a grain of / salt of the earth / salt, below the / attic salt / salt away /salt, old—The well-seasoned eatiom of *not being worth one's salt* first appears in the work of Petronius, a first-century A.D. Roman author. It can be found in his *Satyricon,* a satire on the corruption of the prevailing Roman society. The phrase is based on the Roman army's practice of dispensing a monthly salt allowance to its soldiers, a *salarium,* a word derived from the Latin word *sal,* meaning salt.

Salarium, the source of the English word *salary,* was dispensed to the soldiers in addition to their regular pay of denarii, the currency of the Roman realm nineteen hundred years ago. Petronius's use of the phrase was a condemnation of the Roman soldiers who, he felt, were not even worth their paltry salarium. Today, the expression is used to describe someone who is a laggard and doesn't do sufficient work to earn his figurative salt, let alone his regular pay.

take with a grain of salt—Prior to the advent of refrigeration, spices, in addition to the flavor they imparted to foods, were used to disguise tainted foods, and in some cases to preserve them as well. If a person was presented with a plate of food that he or she suspected of being tainted because of its appearance or smell, that person might add a pinch of salt to the questionable *victuals* (see *vittles*). In the same sense, someone might figuratively receive a piece of information *with a grain of salt,* with skepticism or reserve. This phrase can be traced back to the ancient Romans, whose version of it was *cum grano salis.*

salt of the earth—those people in society considered to be the best or most noble; the Lord's children. This term was used by Christ in reference to his disciples (Matthew 5:13).

below the salt—in an inferior social position. It was customary for a lord's table to be set with a salt cellar (from the French word *salière,* meaning salt dish) placed in the center of the table.

Those who sat nearest to the lord were considered to be *above the salt,* while those farthest from him were below the salt and considered socially inferior.

attic salt—dry or delicate wit. The attic in this case refers to Athens, Greece.

salt away—to store away; place something away. Originally, meat was salted to preserve it. It was then stored away for use at a later date.

old salt—a sailor (because he was preserved by the salt of the sea).

sandwich / sandwich board / sandwich man / sandwich panel / sandwich, knuckle—John Montague, the Earl of Sandwich, was Lord of the Admiralty when Capt. James Cook discovered the Sandwich Islands, now called the Hawaiian Islands; but it was the earl's penchant for gambling that caused his name to be associated with the common *sandwich.*

Legend has it that Sandwich, on one occasion, sat at the gaming table for twenty-four hours straight. For sustenance he was served slices of bread and meat, which he fashioned into *sand-*

wiches. However, the earl was not the first person to *sandwich* meat and bread together. Two thousand years earlier the Romans ate *sandwiches,* too, but their name for them was *offelae.*

sandwich—to insert something between two other things.

sandwich board—two sign boards connected at the top that hang before and after a person and bear advertisements.

sandwich man—a person who carries a *sandwich board.*

sandwich panel—a panel in which one material is inserted between two sheets that are similar to each other but different from the center material.

knuckle sandwich—a fist used to hit someone, usually in the mouth.

sardine/scrod—*Scrod,* a word derived from the Dutch word *schrode,* meaning a piece cut off, is actually the meat taken from the young of cod or haddock. A small European fish named pilchard was popularly known as a *sardine* because, it is thought, they were originally caught in great numbers around Sardinia, the second largest island in the Mediterranean Sea.

Sardines, very tiny fish that are preserved in oil and packed tightly in tins, also describes a large group of people or things tightly packed into a confined space, like a can of *sardines.*

sauce / saucy / sauce box / sassy / sass / salsa—In the later Vulgar Latin language, *sal,* or salt, became *salsus* (the feminine gender was *salsa*), which meant a salty seasoning or a kind of garlic-and-salt seasoning. *Salad,* also a derivative of *sal,* originally described salted vegetables.

sauce—intoxicating beverages.

saucy—impudent; bold; impertinent; can also mean smart or trim.

saucebox—a *saucy* impudent person.

sassy—probably a corruption of the English word *saucy,* although there are those authorities who claim that *sassy* is a variation of the West African sassy tree.

sass—fresh back-talk; impudent behavior.

salsa—Latin American dance music. This meaning of *salsa* first appeared in print in a *New York Times* article in 1975. *Salsa* is also the Spanish word for sauce.

scarf / scarf up / scarf out—The scarf that we wear around the neck for warmth is derived from the Old French word *escarpe,* a purse or wallet hung for safety around the neck. *Escarpe* was anglicized to *scarf* and has become an article of wearing apparel.

Scarf also means to eat voraciously and, in this sense, is derived from the German word *schaffen,* meaning to provide or procure food; to beg for food. *Scoff* is a variation of and has the same sense as *scarf.*

scarf up—to eat or drink; to steal.

scarf out—to eat very heartily.

schmaltz—Orthodox Jews use *schmaltz* in lieu of butter in meals involving meat. *Schmaltz,* rendered from similar Yiddish and German words, means rendered fat (usually chicken fat) and has also come to mean something that is very sentimental or banal, such as certain types of music and most soap operas. The use of *schmaltz* to describe the sentimentality of soap opera drama is appropriate since historically soap has been made from *schmaltz*.

sesame, open—The sesame seed is a small corn-like oval seed that was first cultivated in the eastern provinces of India. *Open sesame*'s use as a magic password can be traced to the story of "Ali Baba and the Forty Thieves," a tale from the *Arabian Nights*. In this story, Ali Baba overhears the magic password, *open (close) sesame,* used to open the robbers' den where a fabulous treasure is stored. *Open sesame* has come to mean something that acts like magic to gain entrance or admission to any locked or inaccessible place.

shrimp—Which came first, the shrimp, a small long-tailed marine crustacean used as food, or the diminutive person whom we refer to as a shrimp? The crustacean wins this contest easily, as it is said to be 350 million years old, while man has been around for a mere several million years. Surprisingly, though, small people were referred to as shrimps before their marine ancestors received this same sobriquet. *Shrimp* is derived from the German word *schrimpfen,* meaning to contract or shrivel.

sirloin—One of the most blatant examples of folk (i.e., false) etymology is the fable that attributes the origin of the word *sirloin* to a king of England who was so pleased with a particular slice of beef that he grasped his sword, touched the steak with the tip of the blade, and reportedly said, "I dub thee Sir Loin."

This noble explanation of the sirloin's origin is, as you have already guessed, pure bunk. Up until the 1600s, this kind of steak was spelled *surloin,* a blending of the French word *sur,* meaning above, and *longe,* meaning loin. *Sirloin* is simply an English version of *surloin,* which describes a cut of beef from the upper part of the loin between the rump and the porterhouse.

The English, always lovers of legend, were convinced of the knightly origin of *sirloin.* Accordingly, beginning in the thirteenth century, they also referred to this cut-above-the-rest as the *baron of beef,* which is defined as a double sirloin roast—in truth, a lordly cut of meat.

171

beefeater—a strong, heavily muscled person; a Britisher.

beef squad—a group of tough young men organized or hired for destructive purposes; strikebreakers.

beef trust—a group of fat people; a group of stout women in a chorus line or women's athletic team; the heavy linemen on a football team.

beef up—to add strength or importance to something, such as the human body, a play, or a plan.

slush fund—A *slush fund* has an entirely different meaning from the kind produced by melting snow, although both are derived from Scandinavian words meaning slops or mud.

Slush fund is currently defined as a hidden cache of money used for illegal or corrupt political purposes. This fund's name is derived from the nineteenth-century shipboard practice of boiling up large pots of pork and other fatty meats. The slush (fat) that rose to the top of the kettles was removed and placed into vats. This slush was

172

then sold to soap and candle makers, and the monies obtained therefrom were used for the crew's comfort and entertainment.

soup / soupy / supper / soup strainer / soup jockey / soup, in the / soup kitchen / soup up / soup, alphabet —It is no coincidence that *soup, sup, sop, sip,* and *supper* sound similar. *Supper,* for instance, was ladled from the medieval French, English, and Latin words *soper, super,* and *suppa.* These words described an evening meal generally consisting of a slice of bread sopped in soup on which people supped. Supper is no longer limited to sopping, as *supper* is defined as an evening or late evening meal, or a social affair such as a church *supper.*

soupy—something that is *mushy* or *schmaltzy* (which see); sentimental.

soup strainer—a mustache.

soup jockey—a waiter or waitress.

in the soup—in hot water or trouble.

soup kitchen—a place where the homeless can receive a free meal.

soup up—to increase the horsepower or efficiency of a gasoline engine; to improve the effectiveness of anything.

alphabet soup—a soup in which letters of the alphabet are formed with pasta; governmental agencies during the New Deal known mainly by their initials. Democrat Al Smith of New York said that the government was "submerged in a bowl of alphabet soup."

sourdough—*Sourdough* bread is made from a fermented dough that acts as a leaven, a yeast that produces fermentation and, in turn, causes the dough to rise before and during baking. *Leaven* is derived from the Latin word *levare,* to rise.

The gold prospectors of California, Alaska, and Canada were called *sourdoughs* because they always carried a lump of sour dough with them from previous batches of bread to start the fermentation in successive bakings. To this day longtime residents of Alaska and western Canada are often called *sourdoughs.*

sour grapes—The figure of speech *sour grapes* comes from an Aesop fable, "The Fox and the

174

Grapes." In this ancient story, a fox tried repeatedly to reach a delicious-looking bunch of grapes that hung high on the vine. It was a hot day and the fox was exceedingly thirsty, but as hard as the fox tried, the grapes were beyond reach.

The fox finally gave up in disgust and concluded, in a classic case of rationalization, that the grapes were probably sour anyway.

spicy—The word *spicy* is derived from the Latin word *species,* a sight, and thus an outward shape or form. It later developed the sense of certain merchandise, especially aromatics. *Spicy,* in addition to describing food that has been seasoned or contains spices, has developed the eatiomatic sense of something slightly improper or risqué.

spooning / spoon-feed / spoon, greasy / spoon in one's mouth, born with a silver—*Spooning* means the demonstration of affection; kissing; fondling; caressing. *Spooning* can be traced to a charming old Welsh custom that involved the presentation of a wooden spoon, which had been intricately carved by a would-be swain, to a young lady of his fancy. If the lady accepted the spoon, the two would go courting.

175

The practice of carving these beautiful wooden spoons lost its amorous value and was discontinued after enterprising manufacturers started mass-producing these utensils. It is ironic, considering the origin of *spooning,* that the word *spoon* was derived from the medieval English word *spon,* a chip of wood. *Spon* was eventually shaped into the word and the object we now know as the spoon.

spoon-feed—to feed with a spoon, as a child; to treat with very special care; to pamper.

greasy spoon—a cheap and often unsanitary restaurant.

born with a silver spoon in one's mouth—a person who had the good fortune of having been born to wealth; a wealthy person. It was once the custom of a godfather to present a silver spoon to his godchild. The recipient of such a spoon would have been considered quite fortunate, and indeed wealthy.

spread/spread it on thick—Back in the early days of radio, the word *broadcast* was adopted by this exciting new communications medium as a metaphor for radio transmissions. *Broadcast* was borrowed from farmers, who used it to describe the broad casting of seeds sown from the farm worker's hand. Through the miracle of radio, news and entertainment were spread—or cast—more widely than ever before. It is understandable, therefore, that *spread* and *broadcast* are, in this case, synonymous. *Spread* is derived from the ancient Greek word *speirein,* to sow (seeds) by scattering. For this reason we call a newspaper or magazine article a *spread.* A *spread* can also be something, like butter, that you apply with a knife. But when you literally *spread* butter on too thick, it is often rejected by the diner in much the same way it would be when a person *spreads something on (too) thick* figuratively, an eatiom that has come to mean in an exaggerated manner, or lavishly.

stew / stew in one's own juice / stew, Irish / steward(ess)—The English word *stew,* to simmer or boil slowly, is derived from the ancient Greek word *stuphos,* for vapor or smoke.

stew—turmoil; frustration; confusion.

stew—a drunkard; a drunken spree.

stew in one's own juice—to suffer the effects of one's own actions (see *juice*).

Irish stew—This ethnic stew is usually made with mutton, lamb, or beef with potatoes and onions. Others, however, suggest that true *Irish stew* included potatoes and onions, but had no meat whatsoever, because the average Irish peasant could not generally afford meat.

The final word in this stew, *steward*, has nothing to do with stews that we eat, but is instead derived from *stiga-*, a German root that means a pig or cattle sty (pen), and *-weard*, a warden or guard—literally a pig or cattle guard.

The steward's station in life improved dramatically as the position evolved to include managing other people's farms and estates. In this century, the words *steward* and *stewardess* flew even higher until they were replaced by the nonsexist use of "airplane flight attendants."

strawberry / strawberries, Boston / strawberry mark / strawberry blond—The *straw* in *strawberry* is derived from the Anglo-Saxon word *streow*, meaning stray, because its runners stray in all directions and produce new offspring in the process.

Boston strawberries—a jocular term for Boston baked beans.

strawberry mark—a small reddish birthmark.

strawberry blond—reddish-blond hair.

suave—Foods that taste sweet have been eagerly sought after throughout the ages. As a result of their popularity, the words that convey the sensation of sweetness have been extended in most languages to describe things that look good as well. The Latin word for sweet, *suavis,* meaning sweet to the taste, was also used to describe things that smelled good or were agreeable to the eye. The English word *suave* is derived from the Latin word via French and is defined as a manner or speech that is cultured, sophisticated, or urbane. *Suave* is also related to *persuade, dissuade,* and *suasion.*

The Greek word for sweet, *hedus,* is the source of the English word *hedonist,* a pleasure-seeker.

sugar / sugary / sugarcoat / sugar daddy / sugared—Sugar has been pleasing our palates and ex-

panding our waistlines for many centuries. The
Sanskrit word for this sweet staple is *sarkara,*
which originally meant grit or gravel. *Sarkara*
traveled westward and was flavored with minor
additions to its spelling and pronunciation as it
was translated into various languages.

sugar—money; drugs; money for bribery; a
sweetheart.

sugary—honeyed; deceitfully oversweet.

sugarcoat—to make something that is unpleasant or distasteful appear to be more palatable
or even desirable.

sugar daddy—an older man of means who
spends a lot of money on a young woman (or
man) in return for friendship and—usually—
sexual favors.

sugared—flattery.

**sweet / sweetheart / sweetheart contract / sweetness
and light / sweet talk (sweet-talk) / sweet tooth /
sweetbread**—*Sweet* is derived from the Latin
word *suavis,* meaning sweet (see *suave*). Anything
sweet to the taste is generally regarded as good

180

and, therefore, *sweet* has been frequently used metaphorically.

sweet—something that is pleasant or agreeable to the mind; gratifying; having a pleasing disposition; a form of familiar address considered sexist or degrading when used in a general way to peers and subordinates; good; delightful.

sweetheart—a loved one; an excellent arrangement or thing.

sweetheart contract—a collusive arrangement between union and management officials that is unfavorable to the workers.

sweetness and light—an attitude of excessive good cheer. The English satirist Jonathan Swift (1667–1745) referred to the bee as providing *sweetness and light* because it produced honey (sweetness) and wax for candles (light).

sweet talk—flattery; as *sweet-talk*, the term means to engage in flattering conversation.

sweet tooth—a craving or love of sweets.

sweetbread—the thymus or pancreas of calves or lambs used as food.

sycophant—Some eatioms have been borrowed intact from other languages without benefit of translation and, as a result, no longer look like eatioms. Such is the case with *sycophant,* a word that long ago resulted from the combination of two Greek word elements, *suko* and *phantes,* which literally meant fig shower, but which the ancients defined as an informant. *Sycophant* is currently defined as a servile flatterer; toady; yes person. The transformation from fig shower to informant and, finally, to toady reveals a lot about the customs of the past, which really do not differ much from those of the present.

In the ancient Greek world, the sale of figs was taxed heavily, and fig smuggling flourished. Fig informants, in order to curry favor with persons of power, led authorities to where the illegal figs were stored, as well as to those involved in the bootleg fig trade. Some etymologists claim that the perpetrator was literally fingered or, to be more precise, thumbed by a fig shower who would make the *sign of the fig* (see *fig, sign of the*) at the accused in the presence of a magistrate. The informant of old is very much like his twentieth-century counterpart who informs in order to seek favor, protection, or monetary reward.

T

tamale, hot—While a *hot tomato* and a *hot tamale* are close in meaning, they are different words in the etymological sense. Both *tamale* and *tomato* (which see), though, are derived from the Nahuatl language of the Uto-Aztecan tribes of Mexico. *Tamale,* from the native word *tamalli,* actually describes an ancient dish composed of seasoned minced meat (and perhaps tomatoes) covered in crushed maize (cornmeal) dough, wrapped in corn husks, and then steamed. There is always that possibility that *tamale* was an ancient variant of *tomato* (*tamatl*).

The *hot tamale* eatiom is somewhat ambivalent, since on the one hand it describes a sexy woman, while at the same time it can mean a bright or capable man.

tea, high / tea / tea party / tea pad—*High tea* has become the late-afternoon equivalent of *brunch* and is defined by the British as an early-evening

or late-afternoon meal similar to a light supper.
The word *tea* has been steeped into several slang
phrases, which have, perhaps, given a new meaning to the term *high tea.*

tea (also **T**)—marijuana.

tea party—a gathering for the purpose of
smoking marijuana or the taking of other
drugs.

tea pad—a place where a tea party (see above)
is held.

tenderloin—The *tenderloin,* located under the
short rib, is the most tender part of a loin of beef
or pork. But *tenderloin* is also used to describe
any part of a big city in which there is much graft
and corruption.

In the 1880s the *Tenderloin* was the name of a
New York City police district (Twenty-ninth Precinct), which extended from Madison Square at
Twenty-third Street to Longacre Square at Forty-
second Street, east of Broadway. At the time, it
was an area in which vice and graft were commonplace.

The Tenderloin's reputation was so well

known, according to lexicographers William and Mary Morris, that "one police captain, being transferred there from a Wall Street precinct, remarked in anticipation: 'I've had nothing but chuck for a long time, but now I'm going to get some tenderloin.' "

tidbit—A *tidbit* can be a small piece or morsel of food, as well as an interesting bit of just about anything, especially gossip. The first element of this term—*tid* or *tit*—is derived from a Scandinavian word meaning a very small object, or a child's word for a small thing, a bit, a small piece. *Tid* can also be attributed to *tide,* and perhaps *tidbit* at one time meant a bit of anything that washes ashore with the tide.

toast / toast of the town / toastmaster—There is a recurring tale of a young beauty from Bath, England, who in 1649 was taking the waters at that ancient spa when a group of young blades passed by. All of the men in question toasted her with the water in which she was bathing, save one, who preferred the *toast* (the lady in question) herself. The young lady in that story then became the *toast of the town.*

The use of the word *toast,* in the context of honoring a person, can be traced to the practice of putting a spiced piece of toast in a glass of liquor. Eventually the toast in the glass was transferred to the act of honoring a person in this way. A *toastmaster* was someone adept at, or frequently called upon for, presenting such toasts. *Toast,* in the vernacular of youthful slang, has also developed the sense of excellent; wonderful.

tomato—This vegetable (actually a fruit) was first cultivated in Central America, but spread to the north and south long before Columbus arrived. The Spaniards brought tomato seeds back with them to the Continent, where Europeans were fascinated by the tomato, which they raised first as a decoration and later for its presumed aphrodisiacal qualities. It was from the latter use that the tomato was known as a "love apple." English colonists brought the seeds with them to Virginia, where they considered tomatoes to be a good source of food.

The word *tomato* is derived from the Nahuatl word *tamatl* (see *tamale*). The final *o* was substituted for the *l* by Europeans, who probably fashioned it after the word *potato. Tomato* is a slang word for a pretty young woman and is also used as a synonym for a baseball.

treacle/syrup—*Treacle* is drawn from the Greek word *theriake,* an antidote against poisonous bites by animals. Later, beginning in the sixteenth century, medical charlatans added sugar or molasses to medicines meant to be taken internally in order to make them more palatable. Thereafter, *treacle* began its lexicographical metamorphosis from a poison's antidote to something very sweet.

Today, *treacle* is a mixture of molasses and corn syrup. Eatiomatically, *treacle* has come to mean something that is too sentimental; cloyingly sweet; syrupy. *Syrup* is derived from the Arab word *sharab,* a drink. The Arabs' penchant for adding quantities of sugar to their drinks probably led to its current sweet sense.

tripe—Foods that are considered by most people to be low on the taste or nutrition scale often develop a pejorative eatiomatic sense. Examples include *applesauce* and *baloney* (both of which see), two terms that have become synonymous with *nonsense*. *Tripe* was derived from an Old French word meaning animal entrails.

Tripe is now actually defined as the first and second divisions of the stomach of oxen, cows, sheep, and goats used to sustain humble folk who cannot afford tastier cuts.

In the sixteenth century, *tripe* was used to describe people who were considered contemptible. But the general modern connotation of nonsense or something foolish did not appear in print until 1892.

turkey, cold—The *cold turkey* call of a salesperson is so named because of the presumed condition of the salesperson's skin while making a *cold call:* clammy with goose bumps all over, like a plucked turkey just prior to its being popped into the oven.

The *cold turkey* call is a piece of cake compared to the effort required to abruptly stop taking addictive substances such as drugs, alcohol, or tobacco. The slang phrase for a sudden withdrawal of these substances is to go *cold turkey*. The reference, once again, is to the appearance of the addict's skin in such cases, like that of a turkey just before it is cooked.

turkey (theatrical) / turkey—If you enjoy the theater and live in New York City (or any other large metropolitan area), you have probably seen a few theatrical *turkeys,* plays that flop or simply don't get off the ground financially.

The theatrical eatiom is probably related to an older and more common meaning of *turkey:* a naive or stupid person; a person or thing with little appeal; a loser or dud. These derogatory sentiments probably stem from the fact that hunters consider turkeys to be easily deceived. And, in fact, turkeys are known to be among the less intelligent of our feathered friends.

There is another interesting explanation for the origin of the derogatory theatrical *turkey* expression. There once was a dreadful play called *To Cage a Turkey,* which closed on opening night. After this *fowl* production, theater people began referring to all stage flops as *turkeys.*

turkey, talk / turkey, Cape Cod—When we get to talking seriously about a business matter or even a personal one, we are said to *talk turkey,* an eatiom that means to speak frankly; to mean business; to make decisions on key issues in a dispute or business matter. The special eatiomatic honor

189

reserved for the turkey alone is due no doubt to its popularity as a main course at holiday meals.

Cape Cod turkey is a euphemism for codfish, a fish that is cheap and in plentiful supply on the shores of New England. The eatiom *Cape Cod turkey* is used in the same sense as *Welsh rarebit* and *Billingsgate Pheasant,* a fish.

turnip / turnip head / turnip (stone), can't get blood out of a—The *turnip,* a member of the mustard family, has edible tuberous roots that were very popular with the ancient Greeks and Romans. The name for this tuberous comestible combines two elements: *turn-,* derived from the Latin word *tornare,* to turn (its shape suggests that the *turnip* was turned on a lathe); and *-nip,* derived from a medieval English word for *turnip, nepe.*

The turnip's shape accounts for the following eatioms: *turnip head,* a stupid person, and *turnip,* a thick silver pocket watch. *Can't get blood out of a turnip (stone),* which is certainly true enough, has come to mean that one should not seek assistance, especially of a financial nature, from a source that has none to give.

vanilla, plain—The word *vanilla* is derived from the Spanish word *vainilla,* which is the diminutive of *vaina,* a sheath or pod.

There is certainly nothing plain about the taste of *vanilla,* which is very distinctive indeed. But because of its use in flavoring a very plain whitish ice cream to which it gave its name, it has developed the sense of something bland or commonplace. *Plain vanilla* has, therefore, become an eatiom for something that is uncomplicated; simple; unadorned.

vinegar, full of piss and—The English word *vinegar* combines the Latin word for wine, *vin-,* and the Greek word for sour, *-akros* (modified to the Middle English as *egre*), and literally means sour wine, which is what vinegar is, at least some of the time.

The alcohol in wines and such beverages as "hard" apple cider, whether created from natural fermentation or introduced into the liquid, is changed by oxidation to liquid vinegar. The spicy sense of *vinegar* has combined with the jumpy or energetic appearance of someone (usually a male) whose kidneys are full to produce the *full of piss and vinegar* eatiom. This colloquialism aptly describes a person who is energetic, interesting, or entertaining.

vittles—*Vittles* is a rustic spelling of *victuals,* which is pronounced *vit'ls. Victuals* is used primarily by the British and means food supplies; provisions. The Latin word *victualis* is the source of *vittles* and has the same meaning as the British version and its yokel rendering.

waffle—The word *wafer,* which is derived from the Scottish word *waff,* preceded the *waffle* iron that later created this delicacy. *Waff* is defined as to wave (perhaps like a bird); to undulate.

To *waffle* also means to speak equivocally, or to straddle the issues, because of the undulating nature of a waffle, which suggests the sense of uncertainty.

yum/yum-yum/yummy—The first sound that a baby makes is usually the m-m-m-m-m sound associated with its sucking instinct. Children, thereafter, intuitively associate that m-m-m-m-m sound with something that smells or tastes good. This basic sound, so closely associated in infancy with hunger and food, is later verbalized by children as *yum, yum-yum,* and *yummy,* words that signify the sensory delight of the person uttering them.

Z

zaftig—*Zaftig* is the anglicized version of the Yiddish word *zaftik*, something, like a steak or fruit, that is succulent or juicy. *Zaftig*, in turn, is based on the German word *saft*, meaning juice or tree sap. *Zaftig*'s eatiomatic sense defines a person, usually a woman, who has a full, well-shaped body; a full-figured person.

zest/gusto/relish/tang—

zest—hearty enjoyment, piquancy, gusto; something added to impart a special flavor. It is derived from the French word *zeste* meaning a lemon or orange peel.

gusto—hearty pleasure derived from eating and drinking—from the Latin word *gustare*, meaning to taste.

relish—a pleasant appreciation of something. *Relish*, derived from the French word *relaisser*,

195

literally meaning to leave behind, is something added to a meal, such as a pickle or some other condiment.

tang—a strong taste or flavor. The word *tang* is traced to an Old Scandinavian word, *tangi,* a projection on a tool.

T·H·E INTREPID LINGUISTS LIBRARY

PEOPLE SAY THE DARNEDEST THINGS...

"Sir Francis Drake circumcised the world with a 100-foot clipper."

"In 1957, Eugene O'Neil won a Pullet Surprise."

"Illiterate? Write today for free help."

Don't miss these side-splitting treasuries from The Intrepid Linguist Library...

- ☐ **Anguished English** *Richard Lederer* 20352-X $5.95
- ☐ **It's Raining Cats and Dogs...and Other Beastly Expressions** *Christine Ammer* 20507-7 $5.95
- ☐ **Get Thee to a Punnery** *Richard Lederer* 20499-2 $5.95
- ☐ **Demonic Mnemonics** *Murray Suid* 20647-2 $5.95
- ☐ **The Superior Person's Book of Words** *Peter Bowler* 20407-0 $5.95
- ☐ **Remembrance of Things Fast** *Susan Ferraro* 20704-5 $5.95
- ☐ **The Devil's Dictionary** *Ambrose Bierce* 20853-X $5.99
- ☐ **The Diabolical Dictionary of Modern English** *R. W. Jackson* 20591-3 $5.95
- ☐ **Fighting Words** *Christine Ammer* 20666-9 $5.95
- ☐ **Gallimaufry To Go** *J. Bryan, III* 20775-4 $5.95
- ☐ **Spoonerisms, Sycophants and Sops** *Donald Chain Black* 20896-3 $5.95
- ☐ **The Phrase That Launched 1,000 Ships** *Nigel Rees* 20824-6 $5.99
- ☐ **Fumblerules** *William Safire* 21010-0 $5.99
- ☐ **If I Had A Hi-Fi** *William Irvine* *Illustrated by Steven Guarnaccia* 21142-5 $5.99

At your local bookstore or use this handy page for ordering:

DELL READERS SERVICE, DEPT. DIL
2451 South Wolf Road, Des Plaines, IL 60018

Dell

Please send me the above title(s). I am enclosing $_____
(Please add $2.50 per order to cover shipping and handling.) Send
check or money order—no cash or C.O.D.s please.

Ms./Mrs./Mr. _____

Address _____

City/State _____ Zip _____

DIL–11/92

Prices and availability subject to change without notice. Please allow four to six
weeks for delivery.